S0-ADE-435

GARBO, A *Biography*

GARBO

A Biography

FRITIOF BILLQUIST

TRANSLATED BY MAURICE MICHAEL

G. P. PUTNAM'S SONS New York

Library of Congress Catalog Card Number: 60-16682

MANUFACTURED IN THE UNITED STATES OF AMERICA

Contents

Illustrations will be found
following page 128

Prologue

GARBO—that headline is enough to make the whole world prick up its ears, and admirers from Sicilian taxi drivers to Swedish professors will read what is printed underneath, however brief and superficial it may be. It is two decades since Garbo has made a film, yet the interest in her legendary person is as great as ever. It only needs someone to say that he has heard a rumor to the effect "that in all probability Garbo is to . . ." and the news is printed in newspapers everywhere.

She is perhaps the most celebrated woman in the world, for all races and peoples know her. She has influenced her sisters from Narvik to Cape Town and given feminine fashion its masculine touch: jacket cut like a man's, low-heeled shoes, and short hair crowned with a beret.

Even financially, her career has been unique. Her first weekly wage envelope contained seven Swedish crowns; her last contract—made at the end of the 1930's—was for 70,-000 crowns a week.

Speak of Garbo to Hollywood people and they will gesture

toward the sky, as much as to say that she is the genius of the films, and that is a tremendous assertion, even if allowance is made for Hollywood extravagance. One thing is certain, in the artistic world of the screen there are two pinnacles: Chaplin for comedy and Garbo for tragedy.

As that greatest of all personalities of the stage, Eleanora Duse, was called only Duse, so Greta Garbo is just Garbo.

How was it that this simple working-class girl reached these Olympian heights of fame? Perhaps she herself supplies the answer when she says that she has never been surprised, scarcely astonished by anything, for she has a feeling of having experienced everything before. Possibly she is right in her ideas about reincarnation. Just as there have been musical prodigies able to conduct at a tender age, so Garbo would seem to have been born inexplicably mature.

All the artistry that she developed was latent within her; she only had to bring it up into the limelight of consciousness to turn it into art. She never needed to study life; for her it was enough to practice it. And it turned into a symphony in which all voices rang out full and whole.

Chapter 1

THE KIDS OF GÖTA STREET

THAT part of Stockholm known as Söder is a city within the city, a fortress surrounded on all sides by water. It not only has its own rich slang, but its own mentality, humor and morality, and one speaks of a Söder boy or a Söder girl. In the past when there have been disturbances in the city, the perpetrators have often come from Söder, and perhaps not without reason, for the people there have not been well-off, being mostly working class. But they are a proud lot and, living so high up, can look down on the rest of Stockholm.

Göta Street is Söder's main artery. In it are not only the big shops, but the movie houses and dance halls; it is a place of neon lights and a setting for pavement flirtation. One of its side streets is called Blekinge Street and at 32 Blekinge Street there lived in 1918 a family named Gustafsson. It was a dreary street and No. 32 a dreary building. The five Gustafssons were cramped in their little one-room flat, but the parents and three children, of whom twelve-year-old Greta was the youngest, got on well together.

Greta's father had a job in the city sanitation department, but he was often ill and in bed, which meant that, like most other Söder children, the three young Gustafssons spent most of their spare time in the street. Greta could never be bothered to play in the ordinary sense—she thought children's games silly nonsense and always felt too old for them. Instead, she would join one of the clusters at the street corners or study the photographs outside the movie houses. Actually, to go to the movies was possible only on rare Sunday afternoons, when she had managed to scrape up the necessary pennies. There was a little fellow called Chaplin who was wonderful at slipping on banana peels and hitting villains over the head, and a fat man called Fatty who was almost as agile as Chaplin, but not quite so funny.

In the evenings one strolled about looking into shop windows or went to Björns Gardens. No one was livelier or more wide-awake in the evening than Greta, and no one had greater difficulty in getting up when it was time to go to school. The only subject she liked was history and she enjoyed reading *Nils Holgersson's Wonderful Journey* in her literature course, but on the whole she hated school. Big for her age, she felt too grown up to spend her time glued to a school bench. The sight of the classroom with its bare walls, and the teacher's desk like a judge's seat, only increased her desire to revolt. Then there was the blackboard, often covered with a mass of figures that were supposed to make sense.

There was nothing at school she liked better than wiping that blackboard clean, and, being the tallest, she was usually given the job. She would wet the sponge and swish, swish, a few strong sweeps of her arm and all the ghastly figures were removed from the blackboard and also from her mind. How nice the blackboard looked, all black and glossy from the sponge! You couldn't write on it then—not till it had dried. Then it could be boring again, as it was when they hung maps on it that were supposed to represent countries and towns. She could never understand that those splotches and lines could be mountains, rushing rivers or glittering lakes.

When the sun shone outside, she could only think how lovely it would be at their little place by Lake Årsta. The family grew mostly potatoes there, of course, but at that time of year they had some lovely flowers as well: mignonette and ox-eye that she had planted herself. They were exciting plants. You could count their petals: he loves me, loves me not, loves me. They had a little summerhouse where she used to change into her black cotton bathing dress. She liked to swim a comfortable breast stroke and enjoyed lying on her back splashing her foot or moving her hand, watching the coming and going of the clouds. That was the geography for her.

"What's this town called, Greta?"

Greta stood up. She had heard her name, but not the question. However, the teacher's attitude and the silly pointer told her what was expected of her. That silly pointer, thick at one end and tapering at the other, that the teacher used to thump on the floor when someone was inattentive, to bang on the desk with when she was angry, or to point with, as now, at a little spot on the map, a big city the size of a drawing pin. Oh, that would be—"Berlin."

"Berlin? What country are we learning about today?"

"Spain," Olivia whispered.

"Spain," said Greta.

"Well then, what's this city called?"

"Madrid," whispered Olivia, but the whisper carried too far; it reached the teacher's ears and the pointer banged down on the desk, making the classbook leap.

The influenza epidemic of the postwar years had reached Stockholm. Eleven were absent in Greta's class alone. One little girl never came back. One day Lisa, Greta's best friend, had strangely bright and shining eyes. The teacher felt her forehead. "You've a temperature, Lisa—you'd better go home."

"Yes, ma'am."

"Would you like someone to go with you?"

"Yes, please."

Greta volunteered and with a hand clutching the banister and an arm around Greta's neck, Lisa started to walk down the several flights of stairs. But she did not get far before she collapsed. Resolutely, Greta picked her up in her arms and carried her all the way down and out through the gates. She hailed a taxi: "Lisa's got flu and must go home." The driver nodded understandingly.

Lisa spent her birthday in bed and wasn't even allowed visitors, but she had one lovely card with a picture of white roses and HAPPY BIRTHDAY in gold lettering, and on the back a four-line verse signed G.G.

Greta could not afford a stamp, so she had drawn the King's head in the top right-hand corner and put the envelope into the letter box herself.

As long as Lisa had flu Greta took charge of Mirre, a big gray cat that lived at No. 32. As soon as Mirre heard Greta's step, he ran out to meet her. It was tenderness he wanted, not food; for Mirre only ate raw meat of his own catching.

Greta enjoyed the school visits to Skansen as long as she

didn't have to go and look at the poor animals pacing to and fro in their cages in the zoo section. An excursion to Uppsala was another memorable event. The old mounds in which the Viking kings of a thousand years ago lay buried set Greta's imagination working and she was so enthralled by what she saw that the teacher had to call to her several times to get her to come away.

"You know what?" Greta said to Olivia one day on their way home from school. "We'll run away from it all." Olivia looked frightened. "Or can you stand going back there to-morrow?"

"Well, no-o," Olivia replied dubiously. She admired Greta and wanted to do as she suggested.

"Well then, bring what you need with you and we'll meet at the kiosk in Ring Street at eight o'clock."

Olivia was almost in tears when she got there, but Greta was quite certain that she was not going to see that awful school again.

"If you don't want to come, I'll go by myself."

Olivia went with her.

Their freedom did not last long. The police found them two days later at a place called Barkeby.

In those days school discipline and punishments were not as gentle, nor headmasters as understanding, as they are now. There was only one punishment for running away—caning. Olivia wept floods at the mere idea. Greta said nothing, but Alva, her sister, who was her senior, went to see the principal and wept and begged that they shouldn't be beaten and, in part, did succeed in softening his heart. Summoned to the principal's study, the two girls were let off with a severe reprimand and the threat that the cane would be used if they repeated the offense. Greta was as white as a sheet when she came out of the principal's study. The idea that a man could threaten to cause her physical pain agitated her violently.

She loathed all forms of physical violence. One winter day when she was coming back from school, she saw a crowd gathered around two drunks who were quarreling. One was very much the bigger and stronger, so the other was getting the worst of it. He fell into a snowdrift but managed to get to his feet again, and backed up against a wall. Then his big opponent struck him again and blood poured from his mouth and nose. Greta felt sick, and with tears in her voice she called out, "Can't you stop hitting him!" The man's burly opponent gaped at her and growled at his antagonist, "I didn't know that was your girl."

"But she isn't at all," said a disappointed spectator and tried to urge him to continue the fight, but the big fellow shambled off, crestfallen.

The intervention of the twelve-year-old Greta had saved the smaller man, and as she walked on he came after her: "Thank you," he said. "Thanks." It sounded as though he needed to blow his nose, but that was because it was still bleeding.

Greta's father was now confined to his bed and his condition was becoming more and more hopeless. He was greatly attached to his family. As an invalid—this was during the First World War when food was rationed—he received an extra ration of butter and bread, and he pretended to be in better health than he was in order to induce his children to share his rations. The children were very fond of him and Greta was very sad when he died, in 1920. She was fourteen at the time.

Life was not easy for the Gustafssons after this. Greta's mother became a cleaning woman, her brother Sven, who was the eldest, already had a job in a candy store, and Alva found employment as an office assistant. Greta wanted to help too, and thought this an excellent excuse for leaving school. But it wouldn't work. Although she was allowed to take an afternoon job, she had to endure another year of school. She earned seven crowns a week soaping the customers' faces in a barbershop on Horn Street. Of this she gave her mother five crowns. Now that she felt to some extent that she was standing on her own feet, it was easier to endure the lessons and discipline at school. In fact, now she had achieved that contact with life and the world of the grownup for which she had always longed. She had never truly been a child.

In her job, she was dealing, of course, with men, but she could stand up for herself—like most Söder girls she had a ready tongue and also she wielded a large soapy shaving brush!

She was maturing quickly and her movie idols changed almost as rapidly. The previous year it had been the cowboy hero, William S. Hart; now it was Thomas Meighan and Charles Ray, and among the actresses, Norma Talmadge and Clara Kimball Young.

One day she and a companion were standing outside the movie house in Göta Street looking at a poster showing the hero pressing a kiss on the fair one's lips so ardently that one of the straps of her dress was slipping off her shoulder. It was a film prohibited for teen-agers. Greta nudged her girl friend: "Let's go in."

"The attendant knows we're only fourteen—I daren't."

"Oh, come on, don't be a spoilsport. Stand on tiptoe."

When the seven-o'clock performance began, the two girls were sitting in the front row staring at the screen in avid anticipation of seeing forbidden things. They were sadly disappointed—it hadn't been all that exciting and no reason to keep children from seeing it.

Greta loved to act at her friends' houses, where the adult members of the household were seated off to one side to provide an audience. Her favorite role was that of a harem girl, heavily veiled and with a handkerchief across the lower part of her face, so that you saw only her eyes brimming with the dangerous mystery of the Orient. Her girl friends had to play the sheik, but Greta was seldom satisfied with their performances.

"No-oo! A sheik wouldn't bow; he'd just come in, don't you see. Like this, obviously."

The friend usually wanted to give up. "I can't play a man."

"There's nothing to it," Greta would tell her, and make the "sheik" try his entrance over and over again. Then, if it still wasn't right, Greta would take the part of the sheik as well, with the result that she started off by being a dashing and noble male, and then crept up into a corner of the sofa and gave a wonderful picture of shyly devoted womanhood. Her friends thought her versatility most impressive.

If she felt that the performance had been too short, the harem girl would wind up the show by singing. Her favorite was a popular song from a review, which did not always fit the setting, but that did not matter, any more than the fact that she only knew two lines:

But see me up there on the stage and you'll say for sure
There's a girl for whom life is all laughter and pleasure. . . .

She sang the lines again and again, till a prima donna's bow informed her audience that it was time to applaud. Apparently most people thought her performance well worth the small price of admission.

Then Greta discovered what was an almost more enthralling way of spending an evening. In one of the side streets up the hill from Göta Street were no less than two theaters, Söder and Mosebacke, where real, live actors and actresses performed. The actors had their photographs in glass cases displayed outside the theaters. They were all very handsome. but that was partly because they were made up; she had discovered this by observing them as they arrived at the theater about half past seven. They weren't quite so handsome then, but dreadfully interesting!

The stage doorkeeper at the Söder Theater was a nice old man. The actors and actresses began to recognize her and sometimes stopped to talk to her. One evening the doorkeeper let her go in behind the scenes, and she had a glimpse of a fairy-tale world, a world full of excitement and life. And the buzz of voices from the auditorium . . . just imagine all those people sitting there! And the slightly soporific smell of mastic, greasepaint and powder, mixed with that of old furniture and drapery.

The man who invariably played the part of the hero in love with the girl was called Sigurd Wallén. He was fascinating, but there was another actor named Josef Fischer who was even more fascinating. She turned away when Fischer paused in front of the big mirror in the entrance to give himself a final scrutiny and asked her: "Are you thinking of going on the stage?" After a moment she replied: "I don't know if I dare." He smiled at his reflection in the mirror, then hurried off, for the stage manager was beckoning.

As Greta walked home that evening, she felt that something had happened, and yet nothing had. It seemed so queer to have talked with a real actor. And that he should have asked if she intended to go on the stage. . . . Why had he asked that? Did he think she was talented? He had looked at her as though he considered her good-looking. She slackened her pace. The clock in Katarina Church struck nine. A steamship whistled out in the harbor and a train came puffing across from Skeppsbron. Was she to be an actress some day? She could speak to Mr. Ranft about it. He could help her, because he had five other theaters besides Söder.

She gave her mother a great hug.

"Where have you been, Greta?"

"At the Söder, of course. They let me in behind the scenes, today."

"You're too young to be running about theaters like that."

"Young? But, Mother, I'm almost fourteen and there's really nothing to be afraid of."

"Well, anyway, you'd better get to bed."

But thoughts of the theater were in her head and she couldn't sleep that night.

How did one manage to get hold of Mr. Ranft? Was it even possible to speak to a great man like that? Perhaps she could ask Fischer what to do. But she was too shy to ask him directly. Maybe he had only been joking when he asked her if she wanted to go on the stage. He probably would think her silly for even imagining she could become an actress. She would call him on the telephone. Her family didn't have a phone, but her friend Eva Blomkvist's parents had.

One day Eva happened to mention that her parents had gone out to visit a sick friend. That was Greta's opportunity.

She wrote down on a piece of paper what she wanted to say, afraid that otherwise she would be nervous and be unable to think. Pale and resolute, she picked up the receiver and asked for the number. She recognized Fischer's voice.

"Hello, this is Greta."

"Greta who?"

That made her nervous and she couldn't go on.

"Hello!"

"Well—Greta Gustafsson."

Pause.

"Have we met?"

"No—well, yes." Eva, who was sitting beside her, giggled. "I mean—only at Söder Theater, at the stage door."

At last he understood and asked what Greta wanted.

"Well, I just wanted to ask if it would be possible to speak with Director Ranft."

"But he doesn't live here," Fischer said, facetiously.

Greta felt stupid and began to stammer.

"I mean how should I go about it . . . to get to speak with him?"

"Must it be Mr. Ranft? Couldn't you speak with me instead?"

She was now so confused that she couldn't end the conversation quickly enough.

"Well, I see it's not possible. Thank you so much."

Hurriedly she replaced the receiver.

If this was a setback, it made no difference, for actually she had chosen her career at only half the age she was then. Her Uncle David has told how, when she was seven or eight, and they had guests at home, she used to sit by herself under the table in the kitchen. This wasn't because of shyness or stubbornness. If someone asked her why she was sitting there, she replied that she was thinking about what she was going to be some day.

"Have you made up your mind already?"

"Yes. I'm going to be a diva, and after that I shall become a princess."

Chapter 2

A WHITE DRESS AND THE COUNT
OF SÖDER

WHEN she was fourteen, Greta left school and experienced the intoxicating sensation of being a "grownup." With the assumption of economic responsibility went certain rights: She could come home later in the evening and was allowed to lie in bed longer in the morning, for she did not have to be at the fruit store where she was employed before nine o'clock.

Eva Blomkvist once asked her where she worked, and had to be content with the rather vague reply that the place was in Sveavägen (which was more than a mile long). Greta did not like supplying detailed information about herself and her doings. However, even though she thought Eva asked too many questions, she liked her well enough, and one day accepted an invitation to her home to meet her parents, who were rather surprised to be introduced to a young lady in high-heeled shoes and low-cut dress, with her hair put up high. Greta thoroughly enjoyed herself and sat munching Mrs. Blomkvist's biscuits. All at once she said: "I am so pleased to make the acquaintance of Eva's parents."

Mrs. Blomkvist looked rather bewildered.

"Are you really only fourteen, Greta?"

"Yes, unfortunately," was the answer, "but that will soon change."

Greta and Eva were preparing for confirmation at the same time. Though Greta often rang her friend up an hour or so before the lesson to ask what they were supposed to learn, she was always able to answer the questions put to her by the Reverend Mr. Ahlfeldt. Like the other girls she had a crush on him and would have hated to do badly in his class.

For her confirmation present Eva was given a watch, a necklace and a bracelet. Greta, who had just a simple white frock, saw Eva's treasures and said: "When I'm rich, I shall buy myself a pair of big earrings and lots of rings, you'll see." Eva offered to let Greta wear her treasures for her photograph and they went off to have their pictures taken together. She did not like her photograph when she saw it and did not bother to order a print. She was particular about photographs.

The confirmation went well. Greta appeared moved and wept so much during communion that her face became blotchy. Afterward, when Eva asked why she had cried, Greta replied that she supposed it was because it was all so solemn.

That summer Eva went to the country and the two girls wrote to each other. A letter dated July 7, 1920, shows that they were on the point of falling out. The Dalqvist mentioned was a popular variety actor whose acquaintance Eva had chanced to make.

Dear Eva,

Thanks for your letter. So you are in the country and having a good time. From what I hear of your plans, I see that you have plenty of time there to think about the stage. One thing you must tell me: how did you become acquainted with Dalqvist? From the idea I have, I think it will be better for you if you did explain. One other thing I have to say: if you and I are to continue friends, you must keep away from my girl friends, as I did from yours. I'm sure you wouldn't like it if you met me with your most intimate friends and I completely ignored you. I did not mind your going out with Alva, but I realized that you intended to do the same with all my acquaintances. Eva, I am arrogant and impatient by nature, and I don't like girls who do what you have done. If you hadn't written, I should never have made the first move toward reconciliation. And then your writing to Alva. Frankly, I think you're making yourself ridiculous. If you hadn't done that, perhaps my letter would have been more friendly. But now I can't be. If this letter offends you, then you don't need to write to me again, but if it doesn't and you will promise to behave as a friend, then I shall be glad to hear from you again soon.

Yours truly
Greta

Remarkable for a fourteen-year-old to be able to see herself so clearly. "Arrogant and impatient" she remained even when grown up.

Eva evidently replied begging Greta's pardon, for the next letter from Greta reads:

SATURDAY, AUGUST 7, 1920

Dear Eva,

Thanks for your letter. Well, so you promise to mend your ways. Then all can be as before, provided I have no cause to complain again. As for your thinking that I treat you like a child, I only do that when you behave like a child or make yourself ridiculous—that is, when I have reason to, but not otherwise. But we can talk about that when we meet. Just imagine, I have got a job at Paul Bergström's. Oh, my dear, when I am there, I shall long for the days I was able to be at home. Can you imagine it, me a shopgirl! But don't worry, I haven't given up thought of the stage because of this. Not a bit of it; I'm just as keen as ever. If you come home soon, you must start at Bergström's too, do you hear? No more just now. Write some time.

Your GRETA.

The next letter is dated AUGUST 15, 1920.

DEAR EVA,

Thanks for the letter! I thought you were going to come back this month and begin at Bergström's, so that we could go to work and come back together, to say nothing of the fun we would have there every day. And Bergström has a son who is one of the managers and very stylish. They all look at me with such interest there, because I'm only fifteen. If you were to come, I'll bet they'll all ask you if it's true. In the autumn, Eva, you and I must go out and have fun together, otherwise I'll die. I long so tremendously for someone that I can really like. Whenever I'm left to myself, I long so dreadfully for the theater, for after all, Eva, everything I want is there. I feel as though I had been alive for a whole eternity and not at all like a high-spirited fifteen-year-old. Just imagine, I shall be sixteen next month. Not many would think it. I think you should come home soon, Eva. What do you want to be in the country for? Tell your mother that you want to go home and [work]. Write when you're coming and I'll ring you up and then you must come and meet me one evening when I finish at six o'clock. And one fine day, you'll go there and try for a job yourself. That would be grand, wouldn't it? Now I must stop before I start making too many mistakes. You must forgive this ghastly letter. Goodbye. My regards to your father and mother.

GRETA.

When Eva Blomkvist came back to Stockholm there was no vacancy at Bergström's store (PUB) and she had to take a job elsewhere. But she used to go and meet Greta and the two would walk home together. Greta had her own particular route which took them through the big forecourt of the royal palace. Eva often wondered why she chose that way, but knew that it would be a waste of breath to ask. Greta would tell her of her own accord or else Eva would never find out.

One day, as they were walking through this forecourt, Greta said:

"You see, Eva, one of the princes might catch sight of one." Which, of course, none of the princes did—then.

But if she didn't have a prince, at all events she had a count up on the heights of Söder, where one of the characters in the revue playing at the Mosebacke Theater was "The Count of Söder." The count's accent betrayed him as having been born a good bit farther south. He was, in fact, a Dane, a former professional boxer by the name of Kalle Pedersen. He took the Mosebacke public by storm, as later he did other and far larger audiences, under the name of Carl Brisson. Soon all the Söder girls were whispering that their idol had begun to pay marked attention to Greta Gustafsson.

Greta had now abandoned the Söder stage door for that of the Mosebacke. One of the actors there recalls how "every evening we had to chase a chit of a girl away from the stage door. But she kept coming back and in the end got so bold that she scratched a heart on the cement wall with 'I love you, Kalle' inside it. In the end Brisson arranged to get her into the auditorium if she would promise to start the applause for him when he came on."

But he also sang to her, and then Greta, lit by a spotlight

from the stage, suddenly felt the attention of the audience upon her, and she wished herself elsewhere. Brisson stood facing her and sang:

> "Here is the girl from Södermalm
> Slender and lithe as a desert palm. . . ."

After that Greta refused to sit in the auditorium, where she only saw half the performance anyway. She was allowed to remain on stage while they were preparing to go on, primping their costumes, touching up their make-up, warming up their voices. She saw the tension in their faces as they fussed about and indulged their pet superstitions. If any lost his lines there was the nice-looking woman in the prompter's box to help, unseen by those in front. Greta nightly found a place for herself among the scene shifters, electric cables and jumble of scenery. There was a little halo of dust around every one of the footlights, cobwebs hung from the roof, and rats scuttled about in the basement beneath the stage. It was the world of the theater with all its smells and drafts, its romance and realism, and she felt that it was hers.

It wasn't long before Greta knew the entire revue by heart and had acted it all for Eva. First she was a prima donna, then a fat male comedian who danced the Dying Swan à la Pavlova, then she was the charmer, Carl Brisson himself:

> I'm the Count of Södermalm—
> I've noble banners
> And excellent manners,
> I'm full of wit and charm!

Last came two dancers and there Greta had to compromise, by dancing the woman's role.

She was far too wrapped up in the theater and her nerves

began to suffer. One result of this was that she felt the same need of solitude that on so many occasions later in her life was to make her go off by herself.

NYKROPPA AUGUST 27, 1921

EVA CHILD,

I liked your letter and thank you for it. To be honest, I haven't thought of you, for the simple reason that I don't think of anything. I have become pretty indifferent to everything. That perhaps is because I'm not altogether fit. I am quite satisfied to be here and don't long to be back. The fact is that I wanted to get to a place where there weren't so many people, so that I could just rest. I have had my wish very well fulfilled in that most of my company I provide myself.

How are things with you? What are you doing? Write and confess. If you don't, I'll pump you when we meet some time. Yes, your confession should be quite interesting, perhaps. It's so long since we met that I don't know what you've been doing.

I have nothing particular to tell that would interest little Eva. But if you care to send a few lines to Nykroppa some time, they will be welcome.

KATHA

(*alias Greta*)

She returned to her job in Stockholm more fit, though still slightly depressed. She confessed to Eva that her taste for the theater had only increased during her holiday and it was the stage that interested her as a career. Amateur theatricals she thought silly—amateurs had none of the romance and charm of real actors. But when the manager of the hat department asked her to model hats for the new catalogue, she agreed at once. There was some point in that.

One day there was an unusual buzz of talk in the girls' lunchroom. The news had got around that someone on the staff was to play a part in a film advertising the store. As a result, when a tall man with a round childish face walked into PUB, he was met everywhere with expectant looks. The man was Lars Ring, a former cavalry captain, writer of adventure books, and businessman now trying his hand at making advertising films. Followed by the sales manager, he strode from department to department, explaining in a loud voice and with many gestures what shots he would take and how, and causing consternation among the girls by now and again peering at this one or that through half-closed eyes.

When the manager of the hat department reminded the sales manager that one of her girls had done well as a picture model, all work in the department stopped. Ring glared and explained that the female role had already been given to the actress Aga Andersson and "she's lovely enough." The sales manager, however, thought that it would be good publicity if one of the staff acted in the film and wondered whether a smaller part couldn't be put in. "The girl's undoubtedly got a movie face," he said, showing the other the spring catalogue.

Ring sat down at a table and studied the photographs.

Was the girl tall or short?

The sales manager called for Greta Gustafsson, and when Ring saw her there was a long silence. One could almost say what was written of his namesake in *Frithiofs Saga:*

> Ring thrust back his chair from the table
> And one and all listened to the words of the King
> Famed throughout the North.

Ring beamed. "I'll take Miss Gustafsson," he said.

However, when the script was ready, it proved to have only one unallotted part—that of the mannequin who was to wear men's riding clothes. Undoubtedly a man would have been more suitable, but having said that Miss Gustafsson was to have a part, Ring insisted that she and no one else should have it. He was an officer and a gentleman and he never broke his word!

When the principal actor saw the mannequin, he said, "You're not going to have that fat girl in the picture, are you? She won't fit the screen!"

Later, when they had been introduced and the actor proved to be more friendly, Garbo said to him, "The last time we met you weren't nearly so polite."

And the man was quite wrong. Garbo not only squeezed herself onto the screen, but she also found room to do a little acting of her own, sending humorous conspiratorial glances at the camera, as much as to say: "I know the outfit is far too big and made for a man!"

Ring thought she had possibilities as a comedienne à la Lili Ziedner, a fat variety actress specializing in the grotesque. He gave her a part in an advertising film for the Cooperative Stores called *Our Daily Bread*, in which she played the "pastry-eating woman."

Eva wanted to go with Greta to see the première, but she wasn't allowed. Greta was very self-critical even then. Eva, who also imagined herself as a potential film star, was hurt by her friend's "superiority." Greta, indeed, felt superior to most girls of her own age; at times she seemed even more mature than many who were older than she. She called her older sister, Alva, "Little One" and tried to boss her brother Sven, who had already done his military service. Sven had begun taking an interest in a girl at the tobacco shop at the corner of Göta Street. Greta did not approve of her and planned to use Eva to entice Sven away from her. One day Eva came for coffee and while the three—Eva, Greta and Sven—were sitting together, Greta leaped up, exclaiming, "I forgot to pull the boat up!" and hurried away. But Sven was not attracted to Eva as his sister had hoped. On the contrary, he was overcome with shyness and Eva was not clever enough to draw him out of his reserve. The girl at the tobacco shop maintained her position after all.

Chapter 3

THE SHOPGIRL AND THE
VAGABOND BARON

A silent film in one act and several scenes*

IT IS a fine spring day in 1922. A man in derby hat and white kid gloves comes strolling down Vasa Street. He is smoking a cigar and swinging an elegant walking stick in time to his thoughtful pacing. Anyone in the know will at once recognize the figure as that of Erik A. Petschler, film producer. He pats his chest with his left hand. Yes, it is still there, the precious document that assures his engagement as producer and star in a comedy called *The Vagabond Baron*—provided the production costs do not exceed 15,000 crowns. Now, it is generally known that nothing is more difficult than to be funny in a film, so it is no wonder that Petschler takes longer

* Petschler's own account of his discovery of Greta Garbo is just like a script for one of the early silent films.

and longer pulls at his cigar and the furrows on his brow become deeper and deeper.

His immediate problem is to get hold of first-class actors for the main parts. Then he will need three bathing girls to group around him, the Vagabond Baron. He can see them in his imagination, the first short and dark, a bit over twenty, sweet. The second, a tall blonde, the same age, sweet. The third, let's see. Slowly her picture emerges from the clouds of cigar smoke, ash-blonde, medium height and younger than the other two, buddingly curved, you might say, and an enchanting smile on her fresh lips. He stops to look at a pair of white shoes in a shop window; they would look rather smart on his small feet.

A young girl has also stopped and is running her eyes over the display of shoes, while she herself—or rather, her reflection in the window, is being scrutinized by Petschler. Good lord, here is his third bathing girl, the buddingly curved one! He glances at her from the side. Those curves ought to look good in a bathing suit and, as though to confirm the observation, he bangs his stick down on the pavement. When this does not attract the girl's attention, he frees his right hand by hanging his walking stick over his left arm, and with an elegant gesture raises his derby and is about to open a conversation, when the girl suddenly vanishes with a haughty expression on her lips.

Petschler is too much the man of the world to be discountenanced. He puts his hat back on his head, shrugs his shoulders and walks on. Within a few seconds his stick is swinging once more and its owner deep in plans. The last we see of him are his white gloves disappearing in the crowd.

Some days later.

Mr. Petschler is again in the same part of town, this time in the company of two young ladies, his bathing girls, numbers one and two. They are out choosing clothes for their parts and thus need the assistance of their producer, who draws their attention to various articles in the windows. They intend to make their purchases at Bergström's. Like the gentleman he is, Mr. Petschler lets the two girls pass in first through the revolving doors. No sooner is he himself inside than he stops, rooted to the spot. There behind the counter in the hat department is his young beauty from the shoe-shop window.

"Fate!" he mutters, and, taking his cigar holder from his mouth, slowly taps off the ash with his index finger. He stares in front of him in amazement.

The young shop assistant also seems to have recognized him, for she too is staring, but her surprise is rather at the fact that her stranger is with two such charming girls. And that's not all. He shows authority in what they are to wear and he seems to be well able to pay. The wallet he has just taken out looks quite fat.

The young assistant has to ask her senior who the stranger is. When she is told, she takes the most daring step of her life so far. Leaning over the counter, she whispers:

"Would you have any use for me too, Mr. Petschler?"

The wretched Petschler has to use all his self-control not to engage the young thing on the spot. With enforced calm he tells her that they had better meet and then he will see. Delighted, the young assistant agrees, and Greta Gustafsson comes, is seen, and conquers Erik A. Petschler!

It is true that she has to recite a poem for him, but that is a mere formality, for in this case physical proportions are what matters to Petschler. After all, it is a bathing beauty he is engaging.

They began filming by going out to Djurgården to take some outside shots of houses. His finances being restricted, Petschler had to think twice before he spent anything. The loveliest of the three daughters (according to the script) got 12 crowns for each day's filming, the other two 10 crowns apiece; a number of eager amateurs, including Petschler's maid, gave their services for nothing, and Petschler played two parts besides being producer and studio manager.

Made up as the Vagabond Baron, Petschler rang at one front door and, raising his hat politely, asked if his company might be allowed "to film a bit." The owner hemmed and hawed, then said that they might, provided the house did not appear in the pictures. They were luckier next door, however, and there they even found a summerhouse in which the girls could change into their bathing suits. According to the cameraman Greta was quite shy in front of the camera, especially when she felt people were looking at her. She was critical both of herself and of others and repeatedly could be heard saying, "Ugh, how silly it looks!"

At lunchtime Petschler produced a parcel of sandwiches and said, "I hope you ladies have brought your own lunch." They hadn't, and with a groan he forked over two crowns so that they could lunch at a nearby café.

Afterward they were to film the bathing scenes, but as the prohibition against bathing so close to the city applied to film actors also, they had to go out to Dalarö, one hour from Stockholm by steamer. So, early one morning, Petschler gathered his little company on the quay and distributed return tickets to Dalarö. Greta had never been there and felt the whole thing a bit of an adventure. She got hungry even before they arrived and unwrapped her sandwiches, saying, "It's fun making pictures, but one can't expect to get rich from it."

Petschler has often described the filming. Here is one of his accounts:

"On with our costumes and so off to the sites we had selected. I particularly remember how difficult it was to keep little Greta from flinging herself into the inviting water. I wanted first to take the scenes that were to be enacted on the beach, so as to prevent the girls from coughing and sniffling because they had been going about in wet bathing suits.

"I remember one little episode that occurred when our filming took us out to a little island. Just as we were shooting, a sudden rain squall burst over us and the three girls had to rescue their clothes, covering them up with umbrellas and mackintoshes and shoving them under bushes.

"As we others crouched unhappily under our chance shelter, Greta and Tyra in their bathing suits improvised a wild Indian dance in the pouring rain. It was a sight for the gods. Greta had her little whims and fancies even then. On another occasion the girls were supposed to be playing near the water in neat little sun suits. They were running in the soft, dewy grass. The scene was rehearsed several times, but when we took it, Greta slipped and sat down with a bump. There she was, the picture of despair. Her blue trousers were wet and so was the make-up on her face, for great rivers of tears from her mascara were coursing down through the make-up. Tyra at once hurried to her help and with a hefty pull heaved her onto her feet again. Greta rubbed her backside ruefully. Then we found the explanation—a treacherous stone in the grass. By the time the make-up man had patched up her face, the sun was shining again and we shot our scene. After various adventures we were back in Stockholm.

"Greta Gustafsson, the future film star, did not actually outshine the others, though there were occasions when she aroused a certain interest in me. I especially remember how one of the main actors was to play a certain little scene. It was taken over and over again, but never done to my satisfaction, and I was tearing my hair.

"I can still see Greta sitting nonchalantly on the grass, hands thrust into her blue trousers, chin cocked up and her little head to one side, watching the culprit with a calm, sleepy, yet interested expression, her eyes half shut. All at once, more as a joke than anything else, I called out, 'Miss Gustafsson, how would you do this scene?' She turned quickly and looked at me, uncomprehending and startled, as if she hadn't grasped what I said. I repeated it. With a slight, embarrassed smile she got slowly to her feet and walked up heavily and awkwardly to do what for her was a difficult task. As far as I was concerned, it was really only a joke, but— *hast du mich gesehen!*—little Greta managed it with such élan and spirit that I was amazed."

The film got a mixed reception. One critic wrote that the film "cannot perhaps compete with foreign models in the same genre where comic situations and technical finesse are concerned; but, though American bathing beauties may be lovelier and more subtle, our Swedish ones have more freshness and charm. These are . . . and Greta Gustafsson who perhaps can become a Swedish film star. Reason—her Anglo-Saxon appearance."

Another newspaper wrote: "Miss Gustafsson had the doubtful pleasure of playing bathing beauty for Mr. Erik A. Petschler, so we have had no idea of her capabilities. At all events it is a pleasure to be able to record a Swedish film name, and we hope that we shall have occasion to mention it again."

Greta realized that she knew too little about her new job. She would have to learn the technique, if she was to be able to swim in these new waters.

Chapter 4

LEARNING TO SWIM

GRETA knew from the actors at the Mosebacke Theater that the director of the Royal Dramatic Theater's Training School, Frans Envall, gave private lessons. She phoned him and asked if she might come and see him.

Envall was a fine old man. He had seen so many fair hopes come to nothing that he felt duty bound to warn his prospective pupil.

"Have you properly considered the step you are taking?" he asked.

Yes, she had.

"The stage is a difficult career. You cannot count on earning any money to speak of for the first few years," he said, and eyed her simple clothes. She did not reply. "The Training School at the Royal Dramatic is free, I know, but you are not allowed to do any other work while you train. How do you make your living?" She told him. "And if you give that up, can you still manage?"

She looked at him and said, "I feel that I must."

There was in her response so much youthful enthusiasm and readiness to sacrifice, and her deep voice appealed to him. He promised to coach her so that she could try for the Training School. The entrance test required that the applicant act three different scenes. Envall asked which ones she would like to do.

"I don't know," she said. "You must decide that."

Envall chose the role of a very weak girl in Selma Lagerlöf's *The Fledgling*, a scene between Birger Jarland and the strong, determined Sigrid in *Wedding at Ulvåsa*; and a scene from Sardou's *Madame Sans-Gêne*. She was to come back in a week's time with the parts prepared as well as she could.

Meanwhile, Envall fell ill. Being unwilling to put young Greta off, he asked his daughter, the actress Signe Envall, to coach her. Signe Envall has had many pupils since, but never one so inhibited as Greta Garbo. On each occasion she sat for a long while collecting herself. "May I just wait a bit?" she asked. And when she did start, she broke off after the first line. "Sorry. I felt that that wasn't good. Can I begin again?"

"Yes, but now try and concentrate properly."

She blushed. Then she obviously became annoyed with herself, and that seemed to be just what was needed to give her nerves the necessary fillip to set them vibrating. After that, the lines followed each other calmly and without hesitation; she took her eyes off the ground and became more and more animated and her voice rang out freely. She was most receptive and never needed to have a mistake pointed out twice, and she had a good ear for nuances of intonation.

There was one rather touching little episode. One day,

Greta brought with her a letter to a friend she evidently considered her social superior, and asked Miss Envall if she would address the envelope for her because "my handwriting is so horribly uncultured." The deficiencies of her education were beginning to give her a complex. But where talent was concerned, she was in no way inferior. In scarcely three weeks she had learned the three scenes for the test.

When the time came, she was so nervous that she asked her brother Sven to take the day off from the bakery where he worked and go to the theater with her. There were over seventy applicants, so the competition was severe. When Greta arrived, the corridor was crowded. Some of the hopefuls were very smartly dressed, some not; some lit cigarettes and tried to appear at ease, but their shrill voices gave them away.

Greta stood in a corner in her fawn ready-made coat, feeling quite out of her element. This wasn't in the least like the cozy old Söder Theater or Mosebacke. It was all as clean and polished and solemn as a government office and even had uniformed porters tiptoeing about. There were brass plates on which the anxious novices saw the names of the great; everything made them feel presumptuous at even dreaming of appearing in such company.

A bell rang and they all jumped. Then the examination began. There was a jury of five, headed by the director of the theater. They were taken in alphabetical order and the first eliminating tests were quickly made. Some were dismissed after only a few lines. A voice that tried hard to be friendly would say, "Thank you very much—next!" The poor girl would stumble back into the wings protesting, "What's the idea? I had scarcely begun!" "Quiet," the manager would say, and the next would already be on the stage.

A dozen applicants had already been dealt with and there

was now only one ahead of Greta. Greta felt so agitated that she could not listen. All at once, she heard the voice from the stalls, "Well, thank you, that will do. Next!"

Greta just stood where she was. The manager looked at her, nodded. "Go on," he said.

Her legs felt numb. When she finally got going and was able to walk out to the middle of the stage, she felt as though she were walking on stilts.

She forgot to curtsy to the jury and just stared wildly at the first-year student who was to be her partner.

Then he began. One more sentence and it would be her cue. Her throat felt dry; she gave a nervous cough. Then she began. Oh, no! If only she could start again. Her tongue was sticking to her palate; her voice didn't seem to carry. Could they hear what she said? She was sweating with nervousness and wiped her forehead with the back of her hand. Why on earth had she done that? It didn't suit the role or the scene, it was a quite irrelevant gesture. At any moment she expected to hear the voice saying, "Thank you, that will do!" For a moment all went black before her eyes. She saw her home, her mother and brother and sisters. She mustn't let herself fail. She must pass . . . must!

Muffled, as though from far away, she heard the student giving her the next cue. Now! She was borne along by something. "It came like dew to the grass, color to the flowers," she began. Then she forgot her surroundings and went soaring off on light downy wings. "There's no blood in my veins. There is only tears." If Selma Lagerlöf had been present she would have recognized the child of her creation.

The student read on unconcernedly and they finished the scene.

Greta left the stage with throbbing temples and sank down

upon a settee in the corridor. Looking around, she saw nothing but the empty faces of young people, who had drained themselves of every ounce of nervous energy and now could not even introduce themselves. Someone tried to joke: "This is like having a tooth pulled. Without an anesthetic." But no one laughed.

At last they were told they could leave. A list of the names of those who had passed would be put up on the notice board later that afternoon.

Greta waited a whole hour after the appointed time so as to escape the sympathy of the others if she had failed. She read down the list: Curt Andersson, Lena Cederström, Greta Gustafsson. . . . She was all right for the next test.

Anxiously, her mother asked how it had gone.

"All right," said Greta.

"Did you get in?"

"I don't know yet. I've to go again tomorrow."

"Another test?"

"Yes."

Her mother shook her head with misgiving.

The next day it was the scene from *Wedding at Ulvåsa.* Strangely enough, she wasn't nervous. The reaction after the strain of the previous day made her feel slack, almost indifferent. She must just take her chance.

She had a manly youth as a partner and she surprised herself by thinking in the middle of the scene what a lovely voice he had. Then it was all over. How had it gone? At any rate, she hadn't been interrupted. But she was tired and she couldn't have been very good. But Greta Gustafsson was on the second list too.

Faced with the final, decisive test, she developed a really

bad case of stage fright. She couldn't sleep, she just lay think-ing over her lines and feeling her courage draining away.

Mrs. Gustafsson had prepared a good breakfast for her Greta. The girl was pale and could do with something nour-ishing, she thought. But Greta merely bolted down a cup of coffee and then hurried off to catch a streetcar.

The streetcar was full and she had to stand all the way. Everyone around her looked so unhappy; or was it just her-self who was unhappy? *Madame Sans-Gêne.* Miss Envall had said that *sans gêne* meant "without constraint," that is, the woman of her part was completely unrestrained. How was she to manage that? How produce that laugh? It was the cli-max, just at the end of the scene, when she laughed Napo-leon's "refeened" sisters out of countenance. She had prac-ticed and practiced it. Her normal deep laugh was no use. This had to sound like a triumphant fanfare and not like coo-ing pigeons, that's what Miss Envall had said. How was she going to make herself seem lighthearted and superior, when she felt so despondent? But Miss Envall had been satisfied, the last time they went over it.

There was the white façade of the Royal Dramatic Thea-ter. Was she really trying to get on the stage there? She hadn't a chance!

There were sixteen of them left for the final test. Ten would be accepted. They were all equally nervous, and no one spoke. By this time Greta had a raging headache. In the corridor the manager gave her a smile: "Well, how do you feel today?"

"All right."

"You may like to know that the director thought you were good as the Fledgling."

Was it possible? Had the great Tore Svennberg mentioned her by name? She had to keep hold of herself not to give the man a hug. After that she would do the test all right. She would put Napoleon's sisters in their place.

This time she was one of the first to go on. For the final test no one was interrupted, so the proceedings were a little more protracted. Greta had two partners now, to play the Queen of Naples and Princess of Luca. They hadn't studied their parts very deeply and seemed thoroughly bored with the proceedings, which annoyed Greta, yet helped her.

At the end of the scene there was silence, an uncomfortable clammy silence that could have meant anything. She thought she had done the laugh all right.

They were to come back in the evening. There would be an envelope for each at the porter's lodge. One of the others had told Greta that if your envelope was fat, it meant that you weren't accepted and they were returning all your papers: school report, medical certificate and references. If the envelope was thin it contained just a brief statement of when the term began. As she stood by the window, she tried to read on the porter's face what her fate was, but she could discover nothing.

"Greta Gustafsson? Here you are."

She scarcely dared take the envelope. But it certainly felt thin enough! She rushed into the street and tore it open.

"Greta Gustafsson, student at the Royal Dramatic Theater, is hereby requested to present herself for registration on September 18, at 9 A.M."

Chapter 5

GARBO

"I THOUGHT I should die of joy when I learned that I had gotten in," Greta said years afterward, "and it still makes me breathless when I remember that moment."

She began at the school in the fall of 1923, shortly before her eighteenth birthday. Besides elocution and voice training, there was basic work in deportment and eurythmics, consisting of fencing and dancing, both of which Greta disliked. Fencing made her feel heavy and clumsy and she had never liked dancing. She was interested in the art of speaking and voice production. Her teacher thought that the pitch of her voice was perfect and that she must just work on tone production. She appreciated beautiful voices.

The new milieu made her very conscious of the defects in her education and now she was more than ever critical of herself, so much so that it could easily have developed into a serious hindrance. It gave her inhibitions which on occasion were almost paralyzing. Yet, although many of the others were greatly superior to her socially, she was the accepted center of their little group at the café where they lunched. She did not talk a great deal, but she was the dominant personality and what she said was worth listening to.

She dressed simply, almost poorly, in a long blue dress and black woolen stockings, and the others felt sorry for her because she was so hard up. She used to walk the two and a half miles from her home to the theater to save the carfare, and at lunch she and another girl, Mimi Pollack, usually shared a twenty-cent dish. She was worried when winter came and she was faced with having to get another pair of shoes. Shoes cost 18 crowns; where was she going to get the money? All she earned was three crowns a night on the few occasions when she had a walk-on.

The first time she did this, she and another girl stood on the stage looking through a hole in the curtain at the first-night audience streaming in, the men in tails and with opera hats, the women so bejeweled that sometimes you couldn't see how low their dresses were cut. Impressed, the other girl turned to Greta and said:

"How smart and elegant they all are!"

"Mm," Greta muttered, "but even so they have to answer the calls of nature like the rest of us."

When the Christmas holidays came, Mimi Pollack invited Greta to her home in Karlstad. One of the male students, who also came from Karlstad, asked the two girls if they would like to recite at an entertainment being given at the high school there. Thinking that he was joking, they said that they would. The boy left for Karlstad and when the two girls got there a week later, they saw posters everywhere with their names in big black letters. That spoiled the Christmas holidays for Greta. The evening of the performance she was as white as a sheet and the others literally had to push her into the hall. It was so crowded that some people had to stand. The critic of the Karlstad daily praised Greta's voice and intonation and remarked on the enthusiasm of the audience, but the best part of it, as far as Greta was concerned, was the fact that she earned a hundred crowns, which meant she could buy shoes when she got back to Stockholm. There was money for another important thing, too. With a little help from sister Ava, who had been promoted, Greta had a telephone installed at their home.

Maria Schildknecht, who taught at the dramatic school, has often said how repressed Garbo appeared in front of the others. One day, when she asked her to read a passage from Schiller's *Maria Stuart,* Garbo whispered in horror to Mimi, "Who was Maria Stuart? Did she ever live?" Then she kept faltering and had great difficulty in concentrating.

Yet at this time she amazed them all with an audacity greater than any of them would have credited her with. The famous Norwegian actor Halvdan Christensen played a season at the Royal Dramatic and after the last performance an elegant supper was given for him in the mirror room of Grand Hotel. The pupils were allowed to be present too and sat at the end of the long table.

After supper there were speeches and then an improvised cabaret in which the guest of honor himself took part. All at once, Greta stepped forth, quite uninvited, while the other pupils stared in amazement. What was the shy Greta up to? Then, to their horror, she calmly announced that she intended to sing a banal music-hall song, "The Girl from Hagalund." The buzz of voices died down, the arrangers of the evening's entertainment looked at each other and frowned. Then, Greta set her arms akimbo in the best fishwife style and let loose, emphasizing the equivocal points and ending up with a cocky, self-assured toss of her head. There was silence as she began and silence as she ended.

"Who's that girl?" Christensen asked.

"Greta Garbo."

"Garbo? But that's Norwegian! An old, old word for fairy or wood nymph."

After this, her companions decided that there was no accounting for Greta. You could expect nothing of her but the unexpected.

How had she got the name Garbo? Gustafsson being in her opinion too long and ordinary for a stage name, she had consulted Mimi Pollack, who proved to have a friend in the registrar's department of the Ministry of Justice. There the two girls went and looked through thousands of names. They had decided on one beginning with "Gar"—a good beginning they both thought; then their fancy was caught by the "bo" ending of another name, and simultaneously they exclaimed: Garbo! Thus she found her stage name.

What sort of pupil was Greta Garbo?

Neither particularly ambitious nor particularly lazy. She was still liveliest in the evening and found it as difficult as ever to be on time in the morning. When asked about her, the director of the dramatic school, Gustaf Molander, once replied with a smile, "I have very little recollection of her, for she never put in an appearance till my own lesson was over and it was time to go and have coffee. She was gifted, of course; though it seemed as though she did not always dare show it, as though she did not have the courage to be truly herself. But at times it would flash out, especially if something fired her imagination."

At this period they were playing Eugene O'Neill's *Anna Christie* at the Royal Dramatic and evening after evening Garbo looked on from the wings. In the dressing room, the corridor, on the stairs, everywhere she acted the drunken sailor's bride with hoarse voice and trembling hand as she put an imaginary cigarette to her lips. She was bewitched by the part. "I should like to play that," she said then. Later she was to have her wish, for the first talkie she made in Hollywood was *Anna Christie*.

When she was not interested, her indifference verged on apathy. One person who had nothing good to say of her school work was the man who taught history of literature. He once asked her if she could tell him when Strindberg was born:

She thought for a bit and said, "In the winter."

"In the winter?" echoed her astonished teacher.

"Yes, I think it actually was in the winter."

After that, "actually in the winter" became a stock phrase at the school.

Thanks to her maturity and striking appearance she was given small parts after only six months at the school, sometimes even with a line or two to speak. The first line she ever had to speak on the stage consisted of six words: "Excuse me, Count, for being late." That was in *The Adventure*, by Flers and Caillavet.

At the first rehearsal she was extremely nervous. When her cue came, she remained rooted to the spot in the wings, then she rushed in and blurted out her line, reading it from the script in order to hide her embarrassment. The grand dame of the Royal Dramatic, who was on the stage, surveyed her through her lorgnette and said, "That's the most forward thing I've ever seen." She didn't forgive her for being late; but the Count did so gladly. He was Anders de Wahl, one of the greatest actors in the country.

Garbo related the episode to her friend Eva. "You understand," she said, "in the theater you have to be a bit forward. Though that's scarcely very womanly. But then perhaps I'm not all that womanly. Do you know what they call me at the school?" She looked at her with an amused twinkle in her eye. "They call me Gurra."

When Pär Logerkvist's *The Invisible* was put on, she played the part of a harlot and received comment from one of the critics. During the first performance, she learned that the author—then relatively unknown—had been so nervous that he had been unable to wait for the end and had gone home during the second act. As soon as the performance was over, Greta rushed to a telephone and called him up to tell him that all had gone well.

No one who had anything to do with her could doubt her affection for the stage and everything connected with it.

Strangely enough, she was never given a comic part while at the school, yet everyone knew what a sense of humor she had. With the others she could be both high-spirited and maliciously funny, and she was always the first to appreciate a joke and laughed her characteristic guttural little pent-up laugh. The others at the school have mentioned her walk, which was also characteristic; she twisted herself forward, as it were, which was not pretty; it earned her bad marks in the deportment class. But her face was beautiful, especially when she achieved a state of ecstasy and could break through the shell of her shyness and reserve. When that happened, her eyes shone and acquired unfathomable depths.

Garbo's work at the school won her the admiration of

her classmates, which was unusual, to say the least; yet when they began to plan the annual school performance and Garbo was asked what she intended to do, she replied that she hadn't anything she was ready to do.

"But you must appear in something, even if you just second one of the others."

"Then I had better do that."

And she did, playing the old mother in a scene from the Finnish play *Daniel Hjort*.

About this time one of the great Danish actors was playing a season at the Royal Dramatic. His attention was attracted by a beautiful harlot who walked on in the second act, and one evening he asked her if she would give him the pleasure of supping with him after the performance. Garbo accepted. No doubt it flattered her to go out with the actor every girl in Stockholm was raving about, nor was she so blasé that the prospect of a good supper did not offer an inducement.

Supper was served in a private room at the Strand Hotel in true French farce style. The actor was an expert charmer and his conversation was in keeping with the champagne and the rest of it. They became quite gay. At coffee and liqueurs Garbo's host gave a discreet sign to the waiter to withdraw. It was time to proceed "from talk to action." Smiling and sure of victory, he got to his feet—and so did Garbo, saying, "Well, that was terribly nice. Thank you so much. Good-by!" And with that she left the poor man to sip his chartreuse and ponder on the duplicity of womankind.

Chapter 6

FIRST ENCOUNTER

ONE DAY Mauritz Stiller, the great producer, telephoned to Gustaf Molander at the school and asked if he had any girls with movie faces whom he could recommend. Molander had a good eye, and, having been Stiller's script writer, knew his taste. "What film do you want them for?"

"*Gösta Berling*," said Stiller.

In that case there were two Molander thought would do, Mona Mårtenson and Greta Garbo. Mona was a second-year pupil and Stiller had seen her, but not Garbo, and he asked if she could come to his flat at five o'clock that evening. Molander promised to tell her.

Stiller was not yet back when Garbo arrived and she was asked to wait, which she did, feeling strangely relieved and intending to go when she had waited a little while. She was afraid of meeting this man of whom all actors spoke with such respect and who was so influential. (She had recently been to see the film *Erotikon*, which had made Stiller's an international name.) Although invited into the sitting room, she shyly insisted on waiting in the hall, half hoping that Stiller had forgotten her and would not come at all.

But he came, and with him was his French bulldog, Charlie.

"This is Miss Garbo," he was told.

Stiller turned and twisted her this way and that, as though he were buying a cow, talking alternately to her and to his assistant, Nilsson. "How beautiful she is! My dear girl, you're far too fat. . . . What lovely long eyelashes she has! Come in." He showed her into an adjacent room. "Take off your hat and coat, girl."

She did so, while he busied himself with something on his desk, but she sensed that at the same time he was watching her every movement. Then she stood there, arms hanging awkwardly at her sides. "Sit down," he said, and she sat down. Then he began to play with his dog, letting it take hold of his hand and then pulling it across the floor and swinging it around, while Charlie growled delightedly.

"Isn't he sweet?" Stiller said, seizing Charlie lovingly by the muzzle. Then he gave her a quick, blunt look: "What's your phone number?" She told him. "All right, if there's anything for you, I'll give you a ring." As she reached the outer door he called out to her: "You must take off at least twenty-five pounds if you're to get this part."

"All right," she said, to herself rather than to him, and as she closed the door she felt certain that she would never hear from him. She felt depressed and wondered how on earth she was going to earn anything during the summer. Perhaps she could get a job in an open-air theater.

Some time later, Sweden's greatest comedy actor, Ekman,

who was then rehearsing the summer program for the Djur-
gård's Theater, found her in Reinhold's Café.

"Hello, what are you doing here?" he said, sitting down.

"I've been walking."

"By yourself?"

"Yes."

Seeing she was depressed, the actor said, "You were good
at the school show."

"Oh, were you there?"

"Yes, but why did you play an old woman?"

"Perhaps that's all I'm good for," she said and told him
sadly of her unsuccessful meeting with Stiller.

With boyish frankness Ekman told her that Stiller had
given him a film test for the lead in this same *Gösta Berling*
film and had turned him down.

"But you've still got work," Garbo said. "You're lucky.
I'd be glad of an engagement at 175 crowns a month."

The actor tried to cheer her up. "You'll get your chance,"
he said. "You've got a challenge in your eyes that no nice girl
can have."

She laughed. When he had finished his lunch, he offered to
pay for them both. "Thanks, that's nice of you. I had a cup
of coffee and a Danish pastry." As he was about to leave, she
said: "Is there no old woman's part in the play you're rehearsing that I could do?"

There wasn't.

A week later, Garbo's telephone rang. She answered loudly,
and heard a man's voice roaring:

"I understand perfectly well, do you think I'm an idiot?
Shut up and do as I say!"

"Hello," she said, amazed.

"Yes, hello, this is Stiller."

"Good morning, Mr. Stiller."

"Can you come out here at once?"

"Where?"

"Where? Who am I talking to, by the way?"

"This is Greta Garbo."

"That's right. Can you take a taxi and come out to Bås-unda Studio at once? It's urgent."

"Ye-es," she said somewhat hesitantly. A taxi all that way out would cost her a small fortune. He realized this and said, "The company'll pay the taxi."

"Right," she said, "I'm coming!" It was all she could do to keep the elation out of her voice.

"Do you know a girl at the Royal Dramatic called Greta Garbo?" Stiller said to his script writer who was sitting in his office.

Yes, he had seen her.

"Do you think we could risk having her for Elisabeth Dohna?"

The script writer was skeptical. She hadn't made any very definite impression on him.

"I know, but that's because she's so shy," Stiller said. "When you look at her, she goes quite rigid. She doesn't dare show what she feels."

"Elisabeth Dohna is an important part."

"Yes, but she's so beautiful! Have you seen her heels?"

No, he hadn't.

"Just one fine straight line. And those eyelashes!"

"Appearance isn't everything."

"Anyway I'm going to give her a test," Stiller said.

Stiller showed his great interest in her by personally supervising her make-up, to the extent of pointing out that two hairs in her eyebrow were out of alignment. When that detail had been corrected, they went into the studio and Garbo was instructed to get into a bed in front of the camera.

"Now be ill," Stiller said.

She was bewildered and only stared at him.

"Have you never been ill?"

"Yes."

"Well, show it. You've a tremendous temperature and you might die at any moment. You're delirious and are drawing your hand across your sweating brow."

Garbo used to say of Stiller: "He compelled one to do as he wanted. I have him to thank for everything."

Who was this man who came to mean so much to her, both as a person and an artist? Those who were closest to him say that no one really knew him. But, as someone has said, he was one of those people with a consuming flame who burn themselves up while they strive to realize their dreams. They are possessed and never cease building up and tearing down the towns and cities of their fantasy. He was one of those restless beings who are possessed by their art, for whom what they have already attained is nothing; what they hope to achieve, is all. When he eventually came back from America, he fell victim to an incurable disease. A few days before the end, he said to a friend who was visiting him, "You know, I've had a really fine idea for a film, but it will be expensive. We'll have to shoot in both Paris and Rome."

"My dear Mauritz, you've got to stay at home now."

"Home? What's that? I've always been a rover."

It was true. He was typical of his race. His father, Hirsch Stiller, was born in Ruthenia at a time when things were difficult for the Jews. They had to live in segregated communities and the only way he could get on in the world was to abjure his faith, which the Russian government did its best to encourage. As part of this program Jewish orphan boys were often boarded out with peasants, where they received pretty rough treatment, and then, at the age of fifteen or so, they were sent to military schools where discipline was even stricter.

This was the fate of Hirsch Stiller. After working for a farmer for six years, he was sent at the age of twenty-one to serve his military stint with a regiment stationed northeast of Moscow. There he was trained for the regimental band. After five years, the regiment was moved to Helsingfors, capital of the then Grand Duchy of Finland, where Stiller married the daughter of a Jewish doctor from Poland, Mindel Weissenberg. He had six children, of whom Mauritz (Mowscha) was the fourth.

When Mauritz was three, his mother committed suicide, and shortly afterward his father died. The children were boarded out with various families, Mauritz with a hat manufacturer called Katzmann.

At school, he was considered a good-for-nothing by the teacher, but he was the ideal and model of the other pupils, audacious and pert, full of pranks and practical jokes, an expert at mimicking his teachers.

He used to say to his brother, Abraham, who had been placed with an orthodox Jewish family, "Don't bother about going to that old rabbi. Come with me to the theater instead." And when he began serving in Katzmann's shop, all his spare money went for theater tickets. Although he was no good as a salesman, his foster father did all he could to keep him from the clutches of the theater, but when a customer offered to give him a student's contract, he did not hesitate for a second. He was then sixteen.

As an actor he appears to have had a violent temperament

which often caused him to overact. Then, in 1904, there were
disorders in Helsingfors and all males over twenty-one were
called up. Mauritz Stiller was due to report on October 1
and when he didn't turn up, the police went to fetch him.
They nabbed him in the middle of a performance of *Romeo
and Juliet* in which he was playing Tybalt. He was sent to St.
Petersburg where he hoped his weak physique would get him
discharged. He misunderstood the doctor who examined him
and thought he had been released, only to be arrested on his
way to the station and condemned to six years' military service for desertion, three of them in Siberia.

Now he did desert. With a faked passport in the name of
Oskar Rosberg, he managed to get to Sweden and Stockholm. There he got occasional parts and lived more or less on
starvation level. He used to come to rehearsals with a basket
containing his meals. If there wasn't an acquaintance to offer
him lodging for the night, he would sleep on a sofa in the
property room. Yet he was no enthusiastic actor. He found it
difficult to submit to the instructions of producer and author. Acting afforded too little creative, independent work
for his taste and the endless repetition evening after evening
was horribly monotonous for him.

When the movies began to emerge, Stiller pricked up his
ears. There were fresh ideas in this new art form. One day was
never like another; you were continually changing your place
of work and that meant travel, which appealed to Stiller's
nomadic blood. The film was something new, just beginning
to take shape, and he decided that he wanted to be in on it.

After a period of throwing custard pies and smashing
crockery, the film suddenly became an art and authors began
to knock on the door and wonder if they could contribute to
it. Even Strindberg telegraphed to one producer: "You may

film as many of my plays as you like." That was 1911, the year before he died—the same year Sweden's first film studio was built.

Stiller was engaged at the studio, working first as an actor, but when he saw himself on the screen, he said, "No, damn it, I'll never do that again!" And he kept his word, becoming a producer instead. Here his rich fantasy was able to blossom properly. He had all the joy in creation that the new art required and the Oriental's delight in splendor and magnificence. He was always ready to sacrifice a little of the truth to make a point or improve a story. In his eyes as producer, people and everything around him were little more than props.

One evening he and a journalist were sitting in a restaurant. The journalist remarked that the waiter serving them was a queer type. Stiller looked at the man carefully and replied, "But a bit exaggerated!" On another occasion he rushed up to a woman in the street and offered her a film test because her face was "so beautifully pale and thin." The woman explained that she was in mourning, having just lost a near relative. "All right, all right," Stiller said, "but this is really a good part."

He couldn't imagine anyone refusing a part because of private grief. But he had a highly developed sense of the beautiful, the artistically complete and perfect. He loathed all that was ugly and attacked it wherever he found it, even among his friends. He was a strange mixture of naïveté and superior intelligence; he was tender and brutal, mean and generous. He was a strange parallel to Garbo who, for all her femininity, had a masculine streak in her. They were both strong personalities and they attracted each other from the start.

The company went out to Öresund to take the exteriors for *Gösta Berling*. Mona Mårtenson and Greta Garbo shared a room in the hotel. It was an education for Garbo to play opposite a man like Lars Hanson, and she listened like the humble neophite she was when he propounded his ideas about acting, as he loved to do in the evenings. But no one was allowed to talk to her for long. Stiller kept jealous guard over his protégée and that often made things difficult for Garbo.

Stiller considered that he had taken a personal risk in engaging an unknown for that big part and wanted to show that he had been justified. He became easily irritated and sometimes openly exposed her faults so that she should face them. "Damn it, Stiller, I hate you!" she said once. Sometimes he felt that he could only get what he wanted by breaking her resistance, physically and mentally. He would drive her to the breaking point. After some hours of endless repetition and retakes, she would be on the point of tears and ready to give up.

"The part's too big for me," she sniffled.

"Don't bawl!" roared Stiller. "I'm going to get you to do it right."

The scene would be taken again.

"Oh!" Stiller wailed as he tore at his hair. "You move your legs as though they were gate posts! And this is supposed to be an actress," he complained, addressing the bystanders.

"I'm doing as well as I can, Mauritz," Garbo said and burst into tears.

"No, but, Garbo, I only want your best, you know that." An embrace and a hug, tender drying of tears and a kiss on the cheek. It was a daily scene.

Deportment and carriage were continual sources of anxiety. *Gösta Berling* was a period piece and Greta found it difficult to adopt the mannerisms of the Empire. Being fully aware of her technical shortcomings, she was often dejected and felt that she was a failure. It must have been when she was in such a mood that the great Selma Lagerlöf, the author of the book, met her, for she described her as "beautiful with sorrowful eyes. Very quiet and withdrawn." But when Stiller succeeded in getting her properly attuned, she delighted him. "Fine, Greta, fine!" he would exclaim. "Come and have dinner with me tonight."

Stiller's invitations to dinner were a sort of certificate of merit and as such they encouraged her and cheered her up, as long as she did not have to ride with him in his car. There was only one who did that voluntarily and that was Charlie. Just to be in the vicinity when Stiller started off was dangerous, for you never knew whether he would go forward or backward. When his yellow sports car came tearing along, people and vehicles scattered. Once he shot around Odenplan at such speed that Charlie, who was sitting beside him, was catapulted through the open window. There was a shout from Stiller, who braked furiously in the midst of traffic and was almost run over, diving after Charlie.

When they dined together, Greta could talk frankly to Stiller and he did his best to relax and think of other things, but he could never get his work altogether out of his mind. Once he tried to explain how she could best be herself in front of the camera without departing from the character she was playing, and she insisted, not without acrimony, that when he criticized her as much as he did it made her stiff and awkward.

"But don't you understand that I must criticize you, since you're so inexperienced?"

"Then why did you choose me?"

He told her that he had taken her because he wanted to

mold her from the beginning, before she had had time to ac-
quire all sorts of hackneyed mannerisms. That explanation
pacified her; and when he assured her that her prospects were
so good that she ought to give up studying at the Royal Dramatic and let him make her career for her, her self-confidence
began to return and she laughed happily.

But often, before some important scene was to be shot,
Garbo would go to Julius, the cameraman, and ask him for
champagne, because she felt so frightened. Julius was always
a sport. And then there was Charlie; square and ugly, but
good-humored, and with the best of intentions. He always
had to be near Stiller and shared the latter's somewhat crusty
love for Garbo. However, one person Charlie did not like was
the leading man. Whenever there was to be a love scene between Garbo and Hanson, Charlie had to be shut up. He
would never have allowed Hanson near Garbo. If there had
been sound films in those days, Charlie's protests would have
made many a retake necessary.

There were two things Stiller always expected to get from
others: the time of day—he never had a watch—and cigarettes. When Hanson once suggested that he ought to provide his own smokes, Stiller just answered, "Why should I,
when everyone else has them?"

The film called for a few winter scenes. They had to wait
till November to take Garbo and Hanson fleeing from wolves
across the ice (opposite the windows of the Strand Hotel).
As it proved impracticable to find wolves that would take
kindly to filming, they used Alsatian shepherd dogs with
weighted tails to keep them from wagging and spoiling the
illusion. When the shooting was finished and the film was

being cut, Stiller realized that it was going to be a success for his protégée. He did his best with the advance publicity to attract the critics' attention to her.

In the book, Elisabeth Dohna is described as a "woman of days gone by" who hung around men's necks "as soft as a young squirrel," and on that basis one critic found Garbo too modern and not in keeping with the part. Another considered that as the young Italian, brought from the sunny south, Garbo's brilliant, somewhat nervous temperament was just right. And though she perhaps wasn't always convincing, her ash-blond, exquisite beauty was all the more entrancing. It was perhaps more a victory for her beauty than an artistic triumph. One critic wrote: "In a few years, I expect, the name of Greta Garbo will be known all over the world. She has the gift of beauty, of unique beauty."

Garbo's telephone began to ring and friends and admirers wrote to congratulate her. She became known all over Sweden, but she took it calmly and was mildly amused by her new-found friends' eagerness to take her out to expensive restaurants where they could show her off—to their own advantage.

Having been paid her fee for the film, 3,000 crowns, she felt prosperous and bought her mother a ring. She invited her friend Eva to celebrate—coffee and liqueur—and admire her new acquisitions: a coconut mat, a sofa that was her bed, standing a little way out from the wall. Eva brought a clipping from one of the lesser papers: "Greta Garbo's way to stardom seems clear," it said.

"Aren't you happy?" Eva said enthusiastically, but Greta looked thoughtful. "I didn't think I was quite that good," she replied. "I hope I'll be better in my next part."

She began to read books, went for walks on Djurgården and thought over her new situation while she waited for her next film part.

She seldom went to restaurants, but on Stiller's advice she attended a ball in Saltsjöbaden given for Douglas Fairbanks and Mary Pickford. Her first dancing parter was Ivar Kreuger, the financier.

Chapter 7

THE ODALISQUE FROM SMOLNA

STILLER had procured Garbo's release from her contract at the Royal Dramatic and in return had undertaken to supply her with film parts. This proved more difficult than he had thought. For him the previous film had not been a personal success. Many thought that he had coarsened the story and the author herself wrote that both producer and script writer seemed to have read too many cheap magazine serials. Stiller began to feel persecuted and started contacting foreign film companies with the idea of leaving Sweden.

An acquaintance of Stiller's had written *The Odalisque from Smolna*, a magazine story about the Crimean War that was partly based on fact. In it, a girl of good family escapes from Sevastopol by stowing away on a ship with the hope of reaching Constantinople and her sweetheart. But the ship's crew sell her to a harem, from which she makes an exciting escape. The idea caught Stiller's imagination. It was a part for Garbo. Constantinople, the Bosporus, new people, new surroundings. Stiller was enthusiastic and together with the author worked out a movie synopsis.

Meanwhile he had sold *Gösta Berling* to the Trianon Film Company in Berlin for the sizable sum of 100,000 marks. Stiller was invited to the première in Berlin and told that he could bring two of his cast with him. He chose Greta Garbo and Gerda Lundeqvist.

They did not reach Berlin till the day of the première and he had only a few hours in which to make his star presentable. He did not approve of Garbo's taste in clothes. He bought her a whole new outfit and arranged for a hairdresser and manicurist to come to her hotel.

"It would be cheaper if I went to them," Garbo suggested.

"No," Stiller said. "A film star rings for her staff."

When the hall porter rang to say that the manicurist had arrived, Stiller said:

"Receive her in your dressing gown."

Garbo didn't have one.

"Borrow mine."

"It's too big."

"No one will notice, when you're sitting. You've got to be the great person. And when there's a knock at the door, you don't get up and open the door, but you say '*Herein!*' "

"*Herein!*" said Greta curtly.

"More languidly!"

"*He-r-ein,*" she said, as languidly as she could.

"That's better. Put your feet on that stool. You're tired. A film star is always tired. It impresses people."

The Swedes were presented to the public before the performance began, and afterward all three went up on the stage, Stiller in the middle, and were given a warm ovation. The applause went on and on, and they had to go on singly and take a curtain.

Garbo had to force herself to do it. For the three of them to go on, with her holding Stiller's hand, was one thing, but to go alone and meet all those eyes was frightening. Stiller stood in the wings watching to see that she did as he had told her. Then at last it was over.

"Why were you in such a hurry to get off?" Stiller asked. "You don't know how to draw applause yet, but I'll teach you."

There was a big dinner afterward and when they were about to take their places, Garbo said to Stiller, "How do you say 'I'm going home' in German?"

"Don't you try to slip away," Stiller said curtly, "we've got to play our cards properly now."

Garbo was taken to dinner by one of the heads of Trianon. He plied her with compliments which left her uncomfortably silent. Stiller said something in German that made everyone laugh. Garbo pretended to look as though she were interested in the food, but she found the proceedings interminable and boring.

Someone made a speech. She heard her own name and everyone looked at her. The speaker sat down and her partner said something to her. The only answer she could make was to raise her glass. Gerda Lundeqvist's attempts to act as interpreter only increased her embarrassment.

The next time the waiter came to fill her glass, she whispered to him, "Taxi." "*Einen Wagen?*" he exclaimed, loud enough for Stiller to hear, but despite the latter's admonishing looks Garbo got up, slipped out and went back to her hotel.

The next day Stiller asked Gerda Lundeqvist to take Garbo in hand and visit some museums with her so that she could imbibe a little culture. He himself had no time, he had meetings all day.

Gösta Berling went so well that the distributors earned their money back within a week, and they were inclined to continue their association with Stiller. Would he consider making films for the company direct?

"Well, why not? In fact I have a script here, with a part just made for Garbo, *The Odalisque from Smolna.*"

The Germans weren't enthusiastic and wanted a different idea; but they hadn't reckoned with Stiller's powers of persuasion.

Perhaps the directors didn't grasp all the advantages of the film. It would cost almost nothing; there was no need to wait for good weather, as the sun always shone in Constantinople; there would be no need to build interior sets, as it could all be taken outdoors in the wonderful scenery around the Bosporus. They would need no extras for the crowd scenes, as people in Constantinople had never seen a film being made and would come rushing to be allowed to take part.

The Trianon people fell under Stiller's spell and contracts were signed binding Stiller and his protégée for four years. Garbo was to receive a salary of 500 marks a month. Stiller, well satisfied, went home to complete the scenario.

In the middle of December all was ready. Costumes and scenery were dispatched from Berlin to Constantinople and then one evening Stiller and his company boarded the Orient Express. Garbo was up at seven the next morning. She had always wanted to travel and here she was on the way to Constantinople. Not only that, but she was earning money and going to play the harem girl, the part she had been practicing ever since she was ten.

The Swedes put up at Péra-Palace Hotel where Garbo's Nordic beauty caused a sensation. The others in the company found Stiller naïve in his effort to launch her as a star in Constantinople. The Turkish public had not progressed beyond the custard-pie stage and scarcely knew what a movie camera was. The leading man and the cameraman only laughed when Stiller tried to induce them to bow to Garbo, and the only outward signs of deference paid her was when a hotel guest kissed her hand, and that was not very often, for Stiller was careful that only those he approved of approached her, while he himself laid claim to most of her time.

One of the first things Stiller did was to hire two glossy, new automobiles, one to carry the cameras and the other for himself, Garbo and Julius Jaenzon to drive around in, looking at sites and going into ecstasies over everything they saw —the Asiatic faces of the people, the beauties of the scenery, and the sunsets over the Bosporus. They celebrated Christmas in Constantinople and Garbo received a wonderful fur coat from Stiller. During this period she seems to have overcome some of her fear of him. Jaenzon has said that once he found her sitting on Stiller's knee. She took the cigarette from Stiller's mouth and said, admonishing finger raised: "Haven't I told you that you're not to smoke?"

When the artists' colony in Constantinople had a big celebration at their hotel, Stiller gave her a Chinese costume of brick-red silk with yellow flowers on it. In the early hours she and another of the Swedes danced a couple of dances, but on the whole she was very shy in public.

Stiller had planned to start filming within ten days of their arrival in Constantinople and had reckoned that the whole

film would take about three months to make. However, for
some reason never explained, all the equipment was held up
at the frontier for eighteen days, during which time, of course,
Stiller had to pay for his company, who were lavishly quar-
tered in good hotels. Local credit was soon exhausted and in
order to pay what he owed and keep the company going, he
required a considerable amount of German marks. He sent
the following telegram off to Trianon:

SEND AT ONCE ONE MILLION MARKS.

All was now ready and they began rehearsing a scene in
which the two lovers meet outside a mosque. Attempts to
film this scene called forth violent protests from the priests,
who refused to allow their mosque to be desecrated by being
photographed. Meanwhile there was no news from Trianon.
Another telegram was sent and then an express letter. When
both went unanswered, Stiller departed at once for Berlin.

Several days passed without any news from Stiller, and
then came his letter telling them that Trianon had gone bank-
rupt and that he had been unable to interest any other film
company in his Turkish project.

An industrialist who had lent them money took the
cameras as security and the German legation had to send the
German members of the company home, while the Swedish
actors were looked after by their legation. It was a defeat, but
Garbo did not appear particularly depressed. She had faith
in Stiller. She wrote to her mother, "In two days I shall be
back in Berlin and we'll see what happens then. But it will
all be all right—it's been a good beginning, in spite of everything."

Chapter 8

A JOYLESS PATH

STILLER had not only Garbo, but her leading man Einar Hanson and also Julius Jaenzon, the cameraman, under contract to him personally, and he exerted himself to the utmost to get work in Berlin for his team. Afraid of losing the glamor that his Berlin success had given him, he installed himself and Garbo in a luxurious pension at the Tiergarten and tried to persuade the world that Garbo's fame was steadily growing.

Garbo's faith in Stiller as a producer was unshaken, but she was becoming very doubtful about his business ability, so she decided to take matters into her own hands. She went to see Asta Nielsen, then one of the brightest of the European stars. Asta was a Dane and friendly. Also, she had great influence. She was just about to start work on a new film and asked her producer, G. W. Pabst, to give Garbo a part.

While negotiating with Pabst's company, Stiller nearly wrecked everything by putting forward unacceptable conditions—or were they so unacceptable? Did he, perhaps, know exactly how far he could go?

"You must take Hanson and Jaenzon as well," he told them. "Nobody but Jaenzon can photograph Garbo."

Pabst objected. Hanson he would take in a pinch, but he had signed up Guido Seeber as cameraman and he was the best in Germany! On that point Stiller had to give way.

During the negotiations Garbo was in an adjacent room. She became almost desperate when Stiller put forward two further conditions. Their salaries were to be paid in dollars as well. Sofar, he hoped, was no fly-by-night affair like Trianon! Jaenzon's assistant, who was in the room with Garbo, almost had to stop her from rushing into the other room and demanding that the contract be signed, but she restrained herself. When Stiller came in she said:

"Why didn't you accept their conditions? We haven't even food for today."

"Quiet, child," Stiller said, "I know how to do this sort of thing."

He was right, too. The very next day Garbo was able to sign a $4,000 contract and their bills at the Tiergarten pension were settled.

For over a week Stiller groomed Garbo for her new part. On the first day at the UFA studio he hauled her off to the cameraman and explained the special difficulties involved in making the most of her beauty. Nobody took a great deal of interest in her, except Asta Nielsen, who told Pabst that anyone with beauty like Garbo's must go far.

"Such a face," Pabst agreed, "you only see once in a century."

Stiller noticed that he was not wanted in the studio when they began shooting, so he left. But when Garbo was on her own, she became so nervous in front of the camera that she developed a twitch in her face. They broke off to let her calm down and worked on something else in the meantime, but when they tried again, Garbo broke down and left the studio in tears.

Asta Nielsen has told how difficult those first attempts were. Garbo was worried by the lights. The Germans used considerably stronger ones than Garbo was accustomed to and she felt shy and inhibited in front of the Germans. The cameraman could not stop discussing the phenomenon of this twitch, and the disappointed Pabst wondered what in the world he was going to do "since she hadn't an ounce of talent."

This nervous blinking was the reason why there had been no close-ups of Garbo in *Gösta Berling*, so Stiller had told them, but Pabst refused to believe it and as a result both he and Garbo went through an ordeal before the difficulties were overcome. Garbo was profoundly depressed by the bad results and found it difficult to manage the daily program which called for sixteen hours' work. In the end and to everybody's relief, Seeber found the solution. By speeding up his camera he was able to eliminate the twitch and show Garbo's natural face. This brought about a radical change in her relationship with Pabst. Now, after having longed only to get home, she found working in Germany perfectly tolerable.

Hollywood was beginning to feel the competition of the film industry in Europe. American producers had found it advisable to lure the best of the Europeans. Producers like Ernst Lubitsch, Ludwig Berger and Stiller's old friend, Victor Sjöström were already in Hollywood, as were such stars as Emil Jannings and Conrad Veidt. Stiller now discovered that Louis B. Mayer, the great chief of Metro-Goldwyn-

Mayer, was in Berlin scouting for talent and that he had been impressed by *Gösta Berling*. As soon as he had signed the fat contract with Sofar, Stiller established himself at the luxurious Hotel Esplanade, where he occupied a suite usually reserved for royalty. He had a friend, a Berlin impresario, who knew Mayer's contact man, and it was through the latter that Mayer was told that by a fortunate chance the "great Swedish master director" happened to be in Berlin and was staying at the Esplanade. Mayer sent up his card and asked to see Stiller. Stiller replied that he would be interested in meeting Mayer, but that it was so difficult to find the time. It was only after additional effort by the contact man and fresh approaches that a meeting was arranged with the great film magnate, a stocky little man with gentle, vague gestures and the voice of a dictator.

What did Mr. Mayer want? Stiller asked, preoccupied. Oh, to go to America. . . . He shook his head doubtfully. But Mayer was an expert negotiator too and he asked what salary Stiller would want. Stiller mentioned an astronomical figure, which Mayer at once accepted. Almost taken aback, Stiller said, "And what about Garbo?"

Who was Garbo?

The girl who played Elisabeth Dohna.

Mayer declared that M-G-M had dozens of girls far more beautiful than Garbo.

"Of course," Stiller agreed, "beauty by the yard, but Garbo is beautiful in a personal way and she has talent."

No, the only actor in *Gösta Berling* who had attracted Mayer's notice was Lars Hanson.

Well, Stiller would not consider any offer unless Garbo was engaged as well. Stiller then did something that was really daring. He let Louis B. Mayer go.

Two days passed during which Mayer cabled Victor Sjö-ström, who was employed by Metro, to ask what he thought of Stiller. Sjöström answered, "All the good that can be put in a cable."

On the third day Mayer invited Stiller to dine in the Esplanade's dining room. Stiller asked to be allowed to bring Garbo, certain that her presence would rid Mayer of his doubts. But, although Garbo sat next to him, Mayer addressed himself solely to Stiller and presented him with a contract running from July 1, 1925, with a salary of $1,000 a week.

"And Garbo?" Stiller persisted.

Well, if Garbo's engagement was an ultimatum, he would suggest a trial contract with a starting salary of $350 a week.

Garbo found the situation rather unpleasant and shifted in her chair. Stiller, however, was compelled to accept those conditions. By way of explanation, Mayer said to her in English, "You see, Miss Garbo, American men don't like fat women."

"Ja, ja," said Garbo, who had not understood a word.

Garbo had begun to like Berlin. She had now learned a little German and could talk with her companions. So, when she discovered that Pabst's initial skeptical attitude toward her had changed to one of definite enthusiasm she took the opportunity to ask him about the possibility of her continuing to make films in Berlin, which was so near home and Stockholm, while America lay in a different hemisphere. Her terms, as she told Pabst, were no less than 2,000 marks a month and the right to live in Sweden when she was not making the three films a year that she was prepared to agree to.

Nothing came of this, however, because Sofar would not pay such a salary and Pabst could not interest any of the other companies in the project. Then Hanson, who did not know about the American plan, happened to remark to Stiller that Garbo had begun to feel so at home in Berlin that she was thinking of staying on there. Having thus learned of her negotiations with Pabst, Stiller complained bitterly, "Here am I trying to arrange a future for you in America and you go behind my back and negotiate with others."

He refused to listen to Garbo's explanation that she had just been investigating possibilities, and packed his bags and went back to Stockholm.

Filming continued. In her spare time, Garbo used to go for walks along Unter den Linden, her sauntering gait making her a conspicuous figure amidst the rushing Berliners. Sometimes she would sit over a cup of coffee at Rumpelmeyer's and ponder life and her situation. The others on the set used to laugh at her for being so partial to Unter den Linden, to which she replied that there at least she could never get lost.

As soon as she had finished making the film, she went to Stockholm, a few days ahead of Hanson, who still had some work to do. Garbo's conscience was bothering her about Stiller. The moment she arrived, she made repeated attempts to reach him by phone, without success.

Christmas had come around again. On the afternoon of Christmas Day itself Garbo called up her old school friend Lisa and arranged to meet her. Garbo was wearing the fur coat Stiller had given her and a new hat, and Lisa clapped her hands together when she saw her and exclaimed, "Oh, Greta, how elegant you are!"

"Pah!" said Greta deprecatingly. "How are you, little Lisa?"

"Oh, I'm fine. And you?"

"All right."

"I haven't met you since—"

Garbo interrupted her, "Well, I've been dreadfully busy."

"Have you?"

From a window came the sound of phonograph music—some popular tune. Lisa hummed a bar or two of it.

"What presents have you had?" Greta asked.

"Oh, this boa. But you have a fur coat!" She stroked it admiringly.

"No, that's old." She pulled a paper bag from her pocket. "Have a ginger cookie? Mother made them—they're good."

As Lisa munched, she slyly surveyed her friend. This wasn't the Greta who used to be so easy to talk with.

"Aren't you awfully happy at being a great movie star?"

Greta gave her hand a squeeze.

"Dear Lisa, don't let's talk about films; it's not everything people imagine it to be, you know."

"Isn't it?"

A church clock struck six. The roof of the church was covered with snow and its façade was festooned with Christmas lights.

"I expect you think it strange of me to ring you up on this of all days, but we had visitors at home and it suddenly struck me how pointless everything was, and I felt that I wanted to have a talk with you."

"I understand," Lisa said.

"Can we go somewhere, where we can sit and talk?"

"Well, we have people in too, but it's only my grandmother and cousin."

"No, I mean to some restaurant."

"But you know everything's closed today!"

"I didn't think about that." She stopped. "Let's go into the church here."

Lisa looked at her and followed her in silence. Neither then, nor on their way home, did Lisa like to ask what was wrong. She realized that it was something connected with Garbo's work. Suddenly Greta said, "Have you seen any of my films?"

"Yes, of course!"

"What did you think of me?"

"What did I think? I thought you were terrific, so natural."

When they reached Lisa's door, Garbo held out her hand. "Thanks, Lisa, for your kind words."

"Won't you come up and have a glass of mulled wine? We won't bother about the others. We can just sit and chat."

"It's nice of you, but I don't think I will. I'm a bit tired, you see, so I think I'll just take a taxi home. . . ."

When all attempts to contact Stiller failed, Garbo went out one day to Lidingö, where he had his villa, a cross between hunting lodge and farmhouse, to try and see him. She had to walk half an hour through the slush from the end of the streetcar line and when she arrived, it was only to find that an old friend of Stiller's, Alma Söderhjelm, was living in the house, while Stiller was occupying her flat in Stockholm.

"I'm Greta," Garbo said when the door opened.

"I know that," Alma said, "and a good deal more."

About a year ago, she told Garbo, Stiller had come into her flat and asked if he might use the telephone. He had held a very animated conversation, sometimes leaping out of his chair, gesticulating, alternately groaning, threatening and beseeching. When he had finished he sank into an armchair and said, "I've just done something that perhaps I shall regret. I've got Garbo released from her contract with the Royal Dramatic."

Garbo asked if Stiller had said anything about going to

America and was told that he had said he intended going alone.

Before Garbo left, she asked Alma Söderhjelm to put in a good word for her with Stiller, which evidently she did, for when a Finnish critic went to see Stiller a week later, he found Garbo with him. The critic seems to have been surprised and disappointed by Garbo. Confidentially he said to Stiller, "You're not thinking of taking that dull, silent girl with you to America, are you?"

"You know, it's only that she's shy," Stiller said. "She'll be all right, because she can take my direction."

The idea of going to Hollywood was becoming less and less attractive to Garbo. She was having difficulty about her papers, being a minor. Besides, her sister Alva had got TB, so that both she and their mother needed Garbo's help, and all her friends were in Stockholm. She wrote to a friend in the country, ". . . so you will understand that it is a very unhappy young person who is busy packing."

She even tried to get Stiller to give up the idea of going to America, and here she had allies. The Swedish film magnate, Olle Andersson, had long been trying to interest Stiller in a big European project, telling him that he wasn't suited to America and wouldn't get on there. Then Stiller's friend, the author Hjalmar Bergman, back from an unsuccessful stay in Hollywood, voiced his criticism. "The best things about America are the coffee and cigars. Go there by all means, but don't step ashore." Then the new film company finally came into being with no other than the great Ivar Kreuger guaranteeing it. Stiller received such an advantageous offer that he cabled Metro asking to be released from his contract. Mayer replied, "Quite out of the question."

And so America it had to be.

Chapter 9

WESTWARD COURSE

On a midsummer's eve in 1925 Stiller and Garbo took the train for Gothenburg and embarked on the *Drottnig-holm*. It was a sunny morning as the ship put out through the skärgården, and Garbo sat up on deck watching the land fade into the distance. She was leaving "the wonderful fertile land" of Sweden for a whole year. But a year would pass quickly. Or would it? It was a long time.

Stiller was in the bar talking shop with a Swedish representative of Paramount, from whom he learned that an old acquaintance of his from Germany, Erich Pommer, had a job as Paramount's head of production in Hollywood. Pola Negri, the great Polish movie star, was also there, as was Emil Jannings. Stiller was soon regretting that he had not made contact with that company instead of Metro.

Garbo came and joined them. The bar was full. Some of the passengers were celebrating their return to the States, others were trying to drown the sorrows of leaving home.

They drank whisky, beer, gin-and-tonic, and the women cherry brandy. The children ate banana ices. Garbo tried one but found it too sweet.

A waiter who was pouring water into a Swedish emigrant's whisky was told, "Not so much, for heaven's sake. We'll soon be in the land of prohibition."

"Pola Negri's with Paramount," Stiller said.

"Is she?" said Garbo.

Pola Negri's first American film, *Forbidden Paradise*, had just had its première and was a tremendous success, the Paramount man told them.

"Who made it?" Stiller asked.

"Ernst Lubitsch."

"Did he? That's interesting!"

Pola Negri, the man said, was now being launched in place of Gloria Swanson who, after playing in *Madame Sans-Gêne* in Paris some years before, had married into the French aristocracy. When she had returned to Hollywood as the Marquise de la Falaise, she had been given a reception worthy of a Roman emperor. She was cheered by vast crowds headed by the mayor of Los Angeles. The head of Paramount, Adolf Zukor, handed her a contract with the modest salary of $17,500 a week and respectfully requested her to sign it. The marquise, however, was not in the mood for signing autographs and there was no contract. Stiller was noticeably impressed.

They had dinner, then back they went to the bar, which was as crowded as before, the air heavy with smoke. Greta put on her coat and went on deck. There wasn't a soul there. She strode along, letting the wind buffet her hair. The weather had changed and now the sea was turbulent under an ominous sky. After half an hour, she began to feel tired and went to her cabin.

Her bed looked inviting, but the crashing waves prevented her from getting to sleep and she lay thinking of the tourists homeward bound, the heavily made-up young girls in three-quarter-length skirts and cloche hats who behaved as though they were out for a lark in their own little dinghy. The boys wore Oxford slacks and garish ties. Both sexes had clean-cut features and many wore horn-rimmed spectacles. Hair parted in the middle seemed to be the prevailing fashion.

There was one Swedish-American family on board. The parents, quiet and retiring, spoke in Swedish, but the children, who were in their young twenties, spoke only English, and this in shrill nasal tones. How carefree and unconcerned they were! Where did they get their self-assurance from? Had America made them like that? After all, they were born of Swedish parents.

After a spell of rough weather, Garbo was able to resume her walks on deck. Sometimes, but not often, she got Stiller to accompany her. He was not one for fresh air. And then he and the Paramount man had hit upon a great idea for a film and Stiller sat up into the small hours working away at it. It wouldn't be a bad idea to have something to chuck at the Metro people the moment he arrived.

On the fifth day out there wasn't a breath of wind and Garbo sat in a deck chair reveling in the sunshine and air and listening to the dull hiss of the water as the bow cut into the sea. How blue-black the ocean was compared to the friendly green of the water at Stockholm. She wondered how her mother and Alva were. Such a pity that Alva had fallen ill just after she had landed her first film part. She was so lovely and had by far the better figure.

Greta had no great hopes for this trip to America. She had realized from Mayer's behavior that she had got her contract only because of Stiller's insistence. She watched Mayer when they were signing the contracts. He had kept looking at her legs. She knew they were not by any means perfect. American girls, of course, were very well built. Mayer would certainly not provide her with spectacular parts. Perhaps Stiller could manage something nonetheless. Still, if she didn't succeed, she could just go home again. For she could start again at home, surely? Of course! One mustn't lose heart. She was not going to be poor again; and she did so want her mother to live nicely, and Alva too. She and Alva could make pictures together, when Alva was better.

America came nearer and nearer and the fine weather held. Then one day, about one o'clock, they saw the Statue of Liberty. It was smaller than she had imagined, but the city behind it seemed gigantic—a colossus whose acquaintance she had no great desire to make. She watched the other passengers hurry ashore, laughing and shouting, while she crept down the gangway holding onto the rail and feeling thoroughly out of her element.

One or two reporters had come to interview Stiller. No one paid any attention to Garbo. Stiller thought it strange that none of the Metro chiefs was there to meet them. They had merely sent a publicity man. Stiller looked disappointed. A photographer took a picture.

There was a damp, oppressive heat ashore. The air hung motionless between the skyscrapers, the asphalt bubbled and people looked as though they were sweating oil. A car took the visitors to the hotel, where Garbo collapsed into a bath full of cold water. Stiller made do with a shower. He was in a hurry to contact the people at the Metro office.

His reception was almost a shock. They were friendly and open, but somehow their friendliness was a brake that prevented him from properly playing his part of the great director. Where he had expected an enthusiastic leap to action, he was confronted by a wall of bland smiles instead.

He began a little grandiloquently, apologizing for his prima donna, Miss Garbo, who had not been able to come with him. She was tired after the journey.

It didn't matter in the least!

He hoped that she would be refreshed in the morning, and if so he could bring her along and introduce her.

There was no need for that at all.

But weren't they to leave for Hollywood at once?

No. They must wait for instructions. So far there had been no word from Hollywood.

From what the Swedish interpreter said, it sounded as though Stiller was pretty small fry as far as they were concerned. Their attitude so bewildered him, that he asked to see Mr. Mayer, though he knew that he was in Hollywood.

They nodded indulgently. Oh yes, Mr. Mayer had said something about that Lagerlöf film being good.

"*Gösta Berling?*"

Yes, they believed that was what it was called.

What was all this? Stiller wondered. Did they not appreciate his greatness, or were they deliberately trying to reduce him to mediocrity so as to get him cheaper? In that case, he had his contract. And he would know how to stand up for himself.

He had better withdraw from the scene temporarily and come back when he was better prepared. Perhaps, though, it would be good to remind them that he was already entitled to draw a salary. He thought he was making a good parting shot when he got to his feet and said, "Well, my contract runs from July first."

"Yes, Mr. Stiller, from July first. Good-by."

He couldn't tell all this to Garbo. Presumably what had happened was that their lack of interest in her had affected their attitude to him. He had as good as forced them to engage her.

"When do we leave?" Garbo asked him when he got back to the hotel.

"It's not been decided," Stiller said, and suggested that they have dinner and then go to a theater. It would be interesting to see if they understood anything of the language.

There were many plays to choose from. The new Theater Guild was putting on Shaw's *Caesar and Cleopatra* with Helen Hayes and Lionel Atwill. Noel Coward had started his meteoric career as playwright and player and was himself creating the main part in *The Vortex*, while *Hay Fever* and *Easy Virtue* were also playing. Another young man with good looks was beginning to attract attention in a play called *Hell's Bells*; his name was Humphrey Bogart. Ina Clair was reaping laurels in *The Last of Mrs. Cheyney*; Herbert Marshall and his wife, Edna Best, were playing in Michael Arlen's *These Charming People*, and Arlen's own dramatization of *The Green Hat* was also on.

It was this that Garbo most wanted to see. She had read the book and was interested by the main character, Iris March, played by Katharine Cornell, the most esteemed actress then on Broadway. Opposite her she had a young actor from London by the name of Leslie Howard. Stiller and Garbo thought them both excellent, but if they hadn't read the book, they would not have understood much as the tempo of the acting was pretty fast.

When they came out, they walked part of the way back in order to see something of the city by night. Garbo found the noisy exuberance shattering: the blaring horns of the taxis, the thrusting crowds, the jangling jazz bands, the crowds leaving the movie theaters, the lines of cars, the blazing lights of Broadway. You couldn't go out in New York, Garbo decided, without coming home a wreck. She tumbled into bed exhausted.

Stiller was up early the next morning and at his typewriter hammering out a synopsis of the idea he had had during the voyage.

Garbo stayed in bed late, as she liked to do. When she had bathed and had breakfast, she went about in pajamas wondering how on earth she was going to endure the heat.

The hotel was clean but dreary. Stiller was being economical and did not want to spend much on their accommodations, while the fact that the porter spoke Swedish solved many of his problems. Garbo's room and Stiller's were adjacent and exactly alike. Beside each bed was a shelf with a Bible, and on the floor a porcelain spittoon, thus providing for both spiritual and physical needs. The bath was as big as the bed and in it Garbo spent most of the morning.

Stiller banged on the wall and asked her to get ready for lunch. Reluctantly she put on a dress and, groaning about the heat, went down to the dining room. Stiller tried to cheer her up by telling her that the Arts Theater from Moscow was playing, and said, "We'll go there this evening."

"I understand even less Russian than English,"said Garbo.

"I'll translate," Stiller told her.

The play was called *Carmencita and the Soldier* and the lead was played by Olga Baclanova, a phenomenon of fantasy and sensualism, who was quickly whisked off to Hollywood where she made a considerable success in films with the ex-docker he-man, George Bancroft.

The following day Stiller surprised the Metro people by turning up again with a fat brief case stuffed not only with his new synopsis, but also a complete script for another film, *Hotel City of Lemberg*. The action took place during World War I and the main part was that of a Polish barmaid. "Excellent role for Miss Garbo," Stiller announced.

The Metro people replied that Hollywood would certainly have its own plans for them all worked out when they were sent for.

But this wasn't merely a good dramatic vehicle but also something quite new and original, Stiller told them. And surely the idea was that he and Miss Garbo were to work together, wasn't it?

All such matters were the province of the chiefs in Hollywood.

Stiller realized that they considered him naïve. If only he didn't have to talk to them through an interpreter. He himself observed how ineffectual and childish his protestations sounded when they were translated. He couldn't even persuade them to look at his work; it was all in Swedish, of course, but what the devil did they have an interpreter for?

And when were they to leave for Hollywood?

Still no word. They would let him know, as soon as they heard. "Sure, Mr. Stiller!"

Now, as they held out their hands, he thought their smiles seemed a bit strained.

Garbo had stopped asking Stiller when they were to leave. She realized that something was wrong, if only from Stiller's hectic chase from acquaintances to friends of acquaintances in order to make "useful contacts."

Stiller had engaged a young Swede, Rolf Laven, as his secretary, and Laven was told to take Garbo out to show her New York. In a shop window on Fifth Avenue she saw a hat she thought she would like, and she asked Laven to come in with her and ask the price.

"Forty-five dollars."

"What?" she exclaimed, shocked. "That's a hundred and eighty crowns. Let's go. In Sweden I never paid more than fifteen crowns for a hat."

She had the same experience in a shoe shop. The pair she liked were far too dear.

"In this country you're ruined if you buy anything," she remarked.

She tried to pass the time by reading the Swedish magazines in their hotel and going to the movies. It was convenient being able to pop into the movies during the day and also it was cool there. She wanted to see as many American films as she could; fully 98 per cent of the movies shown were of American origin.

There was Wilde's *Lady Windermere's Fan* with Ronald Colman, who had just risen to stardom, having come to America in the early 1920's after going through all four years of World War I. Garbo had seen him in Sweden with Lillian Gish in *The White Sister*. There was also Rudolph Valentino, the greatest romantic screen lover of all time, in a Russian costume piece, *The Eagle*, directed by Clarence Brown.

Another very successful film was Lon Chaney's *The Phantom of the Opera*, but the young lovers were mediocre. Chaney was also in *He Who Gets Slapped*, and here she found the young lovers interesting, especially the man, John Gilbert. He must be in the same company as herself, since Metro had made the film. Was he in any other films? Yes.

The Big Parade, a war picture in which he symbolized the young American soldier. The final scene of his leave-taking from the French innkeeper's daughter, Renée Adorée, was gripping. There was yet another Gilbert film, *The Merry Widow,* directed by Eric von Stroheim, whom she had seen as an actor and liked because he didn't worry about appearances and wasn't afraid of inviting ridicule.

The most popular female stars seemed to be Lillian Gish, Norma Shearer, Janet Gaynor, Constance Bennett, Colleen Moore.

Nothing of the films she saw told her anything about Hollywood. Either they had been made elsewhere in the world, or they consisted exclusively of studio sets that revealed nothing of the film capital. Hollywood was keeping its face hidden. And still no word about going there. It was beginning to make her nervous. She said as much to Stiller one day at dinner, when he was in a particularly good mood.

He tried to make a joke of it.

"You know what I've always said; film is a foreign word meaning wait!"

But she wanted to know. "Did you expect this?"

It probably wasn't unusual, he said, for them to let newcomers wait in New York till all the preliminaries had been settled in Hollywood.

Hollywood. How strange and remote it sounded.

"It might be on the other side of the world."

"It is a long way from here."

"Why is everything here so horribly large? Look," she said, "even the salt cellar and pepper shaker are skyscrapers."

"You mustn't go and get a skyscraper complex, Greta," Stiller told her. "The only way to impress people in this country is by not being impressed." He laughed. "I have a good method which I adopt when I am feeling overwhelmed. I do this." He took hold of the lapels of his jacket and tugged. "It makes you put your head up and at once you look cockier. Try it sometime and you'll see."

It did Stiller good to meet friends from Europe who told him how good his movies were. Stiller was a child who needed encouragement and understanding. Through a Finnish doctor, living in New York, he met Martha Hedman, a Swedish opera singer at the Metropolitan, and she offered to introduce Garbo to Arnold Genthe, the star photographer who, among other things, supplied many of the cover pictures for *Vanity Fair*.

Genthe found Garbo's face interesting, especially her eyes and her "original forehead," as he called it. He took a series of photographs which delighted Stiller and Garbo, but the people at the Metro office were not as enthusiastic. They disapproved of the way she did her hair and also of the way she dressed.

"But hair and clothes aren't the most important when one's filming, are they?" Stiller protested irritably. "Had they engaged her just to have the pleasure of paying her salary?"

Martha Hedman took them to a garden party given by a well-known New York lawyer, Joseph Bahler. There they met several prominent people from Metro-Goldwyn-Mayer and Stiller introduced Garbo as "the famous star," but apparently without impressing them.

Then he made a desperate attempt to get Louis Mayer in Hollywood on the telephone, but was told that he was not available. That evening he sat in Garbo's room, smoking in glum silence.

"Shall we pack and throw it all up?" he said getting up and walking to and fro. "What do you say?"

Garbo did not answer.

"Well, we'll sleep on it."

He went to his room.

When Garbo came down for breakfast the next morning, Stiller had already gone out. She decided to devote the day to letter writing. She wrote home telling them how hot it was, hotter than it ever could be in Stockholm and more oppressive. Before she left home someone had told her America was a place of orange groves and palm trees, but instead she had come to a stone desert with no greenery at all and no water to be seen, except when you filled your bath. She hadn't really met any Americans yet, she wrote, and she had no idea when she would be going to Hollywood nor how things would turn out.

Then the Swedish-speaking porter rang and said that a gentleman wished to see her and was on his way up. Almost the next moment a man burst in with his hat on his head and a cigar in his mouth. A sharp, sandpapery voice barked a greeting and an index finger jerked the man's hat up and onto the back of his head. With a wealth of gestures he managed to make her understand that she was to come to the Metro office at once.

Shouldn't she wait for Stiller? she asked lamely in Swedish but the suggestion was merely brushed aside. They must hurry. The man wiped the perspiration from his brow, still with his hat on. Resignedly she followed him out into the corridor. When the elevator did not appear the moment he rang, he pushed the button again and again and swore, punctuating his oaths with clouds of cigar smoke. Then the elevator boy opened the doors and they slipped in. Suddenly something most peculiar happened; the man removed his hat! But he went on smoking his cigar and seemed not to notice that the smoke made Garbo cough. He let her go out first, but then strode off ahead of her and ran down the steps. He hardly gave her the chance to get both feet into the waiting car before he stepped on the gas.

Garbo had never driven so fast in any car, not even with Stiller. But the young man could drive—and knew how to use his horn. She couldn't help laughing, and he threw a startled look at the mirror.

Finally they reached the Metro office on Broadway. Garbo saw the number, 1540. Were there really such long streets? They got out at the sixteenth floor and Garbo was asked to take a seat in a waiting room, while the young man disappeared with a great burst of energy down a corridor. He returned in a moment and, pointing to his wrist watch, indicated that "the chief" would see her in half an hour.

Half an hour—then why all the hurry? They seemed to do things at top speed just for appearance' sake. Everything went quickly, elevators, trains, cars, whether it was necessary or not; even the shoeshine stand at the corner near the hotel guaranteed a shine in thirty seconds. Garbo had seen the advertisement of a Turkish bath proclaiming that you became a new person "in one moment"; and a restaurant nearby claimed that you could lunch there in one hundred seconds flat.

She looked around the waiting room. Past and present Metro stars regarded her from the walls, all with beautiful smiles. How had they time to smile, when everything had to move so quickly? But when you looked closer, you could see that they were quite breathless. She herself felt harassed and unsure of herself. If only Stiller had been with her.

The young man returned and grunted something that she presumed meant that the chief would see her. She followed him down a long corridor and then another and so came to an open door.

In the room were a couple of kindly smiling men and— Stiller. As Greta entered he took hold of his coat lapels with both hands and looked like a boxer sure of a victory on points. She was told of the decision that she and Stiller were to leave for Hollywood the next day; they had merely wanted to see her before she went. Knowing that she did not understand English, they kept the meeting brief. They shook hands and wished her luck. On the desk lay a copy of the new issue of *Vanity Fair*, the cover of which was a picture of Garbo done by Genthe.

Their last evening in New York! They slipped into a speakeasy, then considered a show—something amusing. There were lots of revues, one with the Marx brothers, one with Al Jolson, another with Joe E. Brown. In this last one was a policeman played by Walter Pidgeon, and also a good dancer, Clifton Webb. They chose something all English, *Charlot's Revue* with Gertrude Lawrence, Beatrice Lillie and Jack Buchanan.

The next day they were in a train speeding westward across the American continent. Although, after Chicago, the train stopped only in the larger cities, the journey took four whole days. What a country!

Now they were in California. Garbo had not said a word for a long time. She just sat looking at the desert landscape. The first of the palms began to appear.

Stiller looked at her. She was like a drooping flower. The heat of New York had been oppressive and this long train journey had done the rest.

"Well, Greta, how do you feel?"

"All right."

Now they were rolling through the suburbs of Los Angeles. Still Garbo did not speak.

"Remember that trick I told you about," Stiller said, and tugged at his lapels, trying to look like a world conqueror. Garbo just nodded.

The train stopped in Southern Pacific Station. They had arrived.

Chapter 10

THE TEMPTRESS WHO DIDN'T WANT
TO TEMPT

THE group assembled on the platform to greet them was representative enough to please Stiller. However, the occasion was not exactly impressive. A chief of production presented Garbo with a bouquet and made a short speech. The Swedish girl was anything but a film beauty! According to current tastes a motion-picture beauty should be a bit of a doll. In Sweden Garbo was called tall and stately, which the Americans translated as big and lumbering. Was this country girl with enormous feet in low-heeled shoes, with a hole in one stocking, anything to import! Granted, she had lovely eyes, but such an old-fashioned hair-do—and unpolished nails! The photographers began their routine and seemed quite disinterested. This couldn't possibly be the same girl as the one on the cover of *Vanity Fair*.

It is no exaggeration to say that the interest in Garbo was extinguished before it had had time to begin.

A Swede, Erik Stocklossa, who had filmed in Sweden with both Stiller and Sjöström and now was an interior decorator in Hollywood, was one of those who had come to meet them. He invited them to a welcome party at his home. The whole Swedish colony was there (in Hollywood all Scandinavians were called Swedes); they drank cocktails, danced and talked.

"But where's Victor?" Stiller suddenly asked.

"Sjöström's at the studio working on his new film."

Sjöström was then making *The Scarlet Letter* with Lillian Gish and that day they were shooting crowd scenes in the big studio with several hundred extras taking part. The studio covered almost an acre and really was the "biggest in the world." In order to be able to survey this expanse, they had built a platform for Sjöström from which he directed his troops through a megaphone. Sjöström was upon his platform issuing orders, when suddenly he heard a deep voice behind him say in Swedish, "You've got soap on your ears, Victor!" He turned around and there was Stiller. A little distance from the platform stood a shy Swedish girl. "This is Garbo," said Stiller. Sjöström stepped down to greet her.

At five o'clock they all went to Sjöström's home for dinner. While Sjöström's wife, Edith, was getting a meal ready, Garbo sat and played with their two girls, Guje and Kaje, who were twelve and ten. "Guje," Garbo said roguishly, "it's fifteen years since anyone gave me a hug, will you give me a real, hard one?" And Guje did.

"Was that hard, Aunt Greta?"

"Yes, indeed. You *are* strong."

Stiller spoke of his tribulations in New York, and Sjöström, who had now been in Hollywood more than two years, had a lot to tell him about America. California had its dark side as well. "I just go about longing for rain," he said. "To say nothing of frost and snow," his wife put in. They both missed Sweden and only their children were content.

After dinner they went out into the garden. Sjöström watched Garbo playing with his daughters in the grass.

"She's going to be something," Stiller said.

"Do you think so? She doesn't know much English."

"As much as I do," Stiller said laughing. He sipped his coffee and puffed at his cigar. "Well, if one is to believe Hjalmar Bergman, I've now sampled what's best in America, the tobacco and coffee," he said.

"Yes, Bergman wasn't happy here," Sjöström said. "He spent ten months in the script department just collecting his salary. They didn't use a thing he wrote. He was happy when he could go home, and I must say that at the time I would gladly have gone with him. I was here a whole year before I got going."

Stiller looked horrified.

"A whole year! I should go out of my mind!"

"Calm yourself," Sjöström said. "It doesn't mean that it will be the same for you. You are more easygoing than I and you won't find things so difficult."

But there Sjöström was wrong. Stiller was like a race horse and wanted quick results. If he couldn't start a thing at once, it made him nervous and quarrelsome. Where Garbo was concerned, it was like that first period in Germany. Her lack of English isolated her and the waiting became a real trial. She and Stiller did what they could to help each other endure the trying uncertainty. Here too, when Stiller asked when they were to begin work, he was told, "Wait and see, Mr. Stiller!"

Now Garbo sat in a hotel in California, instead of New York. That was the only difference, as far as she was concerned. An assistant from Metro who could make himself understood in Swedish had been told to look after her. He asked if she would like to live in a house of her own or in a hotel suite. She replied that she would prefer a room with some decent family. Somewhat taken aback, he explained that that was out of the question for someone in her position, so she settled for a hotel in Santa Monica, the Miramar, which had a Norwegian manager who could help over the worst language difficulties. And also, as the young man pointed out, it had the great advantage of being only twenty-five miles from the studio in Culver City. Only twenty-five miles!

She disliked Hollywood from the start. It seemed to have been poisoned by the movies. Everyone in it lived for and off films, from the stars in Beverly Hills to the cigar stores on Sunset Boulevard that sold their touched-up portrait photographs and equally artificial life stories. Along the avenues lovely, painted girls hummed the hit from *No, No, Nanette.* "I want to be happy, but I won't be happy, till I make you happy too." And the one they all wanted to make happy was Rudolph Valentino, while they themselves were depressing imitations of various film stars. The palm trees all looked as though they needed dusting and the very air smelled of gasoline.

But Santa Monica was airy. There she could swim in the sea and be near Stiller, who had rented a bungalow on the coast. He was a nonswimmer and looked askance at her long swims. She usually had dinner at his house, and there one day she met Einar Hanson with whom she had worked in Berlin and Constantinople. He had been engaged by Paramount and seemed to be finding his feet quickly. He suggested that they go out and amuse themselves, but she did not feel in the mood. Hanson soon got caught up in Hollywood night life, drank too much and ended by smashing his car and killing himself.

Garbo found it humiliating not to be able to understand what was said to her. She began taking English lessons. She chose a Negro woman to teach her because she felt less inhibited with a colored person. But with her faulty education it was hard going. At the hotel, she dared only speak to the manager. Otherwise, she only saw Stiller, who could not help her learn the language nor entertain her. He spent most of his time sulking.

One day her mentor suggested that they go out to Culver City and have a look at the Metro establishment. At the impressive entrance with its huge gates was a crowd of fans. When Garbo's car stopped for a moment, a boy rushed up with lifted autograph book. He leaped onto the running board and peered in at her.

"Is it anyone?" one of the others asked.

"No. Nobody," he replied.

The M-G-M studios were a town in themselves. They had arrived just at the end of the lunch hour and people were swarming out of the restaurant, actors and technicians and stage hands. There were genuine Zulus, men in tails and women in evening dress, followed by a horde of Indians who, judging by their paint, were on the warpath. Then came a chattering, giggling crowd of ballet girls, taking little dance steps as they went along. They all disappeared into the various studios along the three-mile avenue.

Garbo clenched her hands. Was this where she was going to work? She thought regretfully of the idyllic Swedish studio with its A and B halls. Here there were thirty studios. *Gösta Berling* had taken a whole year to make, because they had to have both summer and winter scenes; but at Metro they conjured the seasons forth as they went along and a film could be made in six weeks, a crazy speed. It was nothing unusual for them to have fifteen pictures under production at one time.

She pointed to a building. Were those the offices? No, the script department. There alone, more than a hundred people were employed and every scene filmed had passed through the brains of synopsis writers, gag writers and script writers before acquiring its final shape. The company had its own electric plant, its own fire brigade, its own police force of two hundred men, direct telephone lines to the head office in New York, dressing rooms for three thousand performers and a total of ten thousand employees.

How big everything was! she thought. Everything, even the sea, which was so huge it had to be called an ocean. You got some wind from it, it was true, but that was seldom much help against the heat of California. Yes, America was a big place and a hot one. It made her giddy.

When was she going to begin filming? she asked. Her companion didn't know, but tried to comfort her, telling her that news would come.

This is what she wrote in one of her letters home:

> You are quite right in thinking that I'm not happy here. God, how I dislike this shapeless country, and if you knew how ugly their studios are, and everything such a confusion and jumble, just like my poor head at times. I live in a dreary hotel in the quietest part and sometimes feel I'm wrong to do it. But one can't live in Hollywood. There are millions of motorcars there—I haven't seen any of the stars here. I dream of our theaters at home that must be opening now. Oh, my

enchanting little Sweden, how happy I shall be to get home to you again!

Meanwhile, publicity had to be got ready in case she was going to be used. The publicity manager racked his brains; what was he to make of the girl? She was big and strong. All right—a sports girl. She objected. Apart from swimming, she had never had any interest in sport. That didn't matter. Clad in shorts and a sweater, she was placed with one toe on a chalk line beside a man with a revolver ready to fire the starting shot. A fine picture! She was made to shake hands with a world-famous boxer, but found it difficult to look impressed. She was even photographed inside the cage of Metro's own lion and the picture was captioned: "Brave daughter of Vikings visits lion in its den."

"I have never been so afraid in my life," she wrote to a friend. "If I ever become as great as Lillian Gish, I shall have it in my contract that I'm to be spared such idiocies. And no shaking hands with professional boxers."

Soon she began to get instructions that affected her private life. She was ordered to take riding lessons in order to reduce. Two of her teeth weren't quite in alignment and would come out dark on photographs if they weren't straightened. Her hair had to have special treatment.

It was only at home in Sweden that one was allowed to be oneself! Hollywood was the city of illusions, where appearance was everything. This held true not only of the humans but of the flowers as well; they were lovely, but without fragrance. She thought that the birds didn't even sing, but just flitted about with perhaps a cheep at the most. But their coloring was lovely. Glamor, glamor, that was the only acceptable currency.

The owner of the riding academy at Santa Monica, Mr.

Seavor, remembers when she first came and asked the price of lessons. Garbo converted the four dollars an hour into Swedish crowns and told him it was too much. He looked at her simple getup, tweed jacket and ready-made breeches, and reduced his fee to three dollars.

She did not always change after her riding lessons, but sometimes turned up at Stiller's for dinner in her riding habit and without a hat on her unruly hair. Stiller had reached the stage when everything irritated him.

"What a sight your hair is!" he exclaimed.

She had brought with her some newspapers and a letter from home to cheer him up. Once she came with a bottle of aquavit, but nothing helped.

"Mauritz, you must take up something or you'll go out of your mind. Couldn't you start riding, too?"

"That's idiotic. I don't need to lose weight."

"It's good relaxation and keeps you fit."

She succeeded in getting him to be "idiotic." Being a person who cared about his appearance, he went to a tailor and had a jacket and breeches made in a shade of terra cotta that went well with his dark complexion and grizzled temples. Complete with whip and gleaming boots he entered the stables, where he was asked if he wanted lessons.

Lessons! He didn't need lessons to sit on a horse. There was nothing to it.

Whether it was his disparagement of the equestrian art that annoyed Mr. Seavor, or merely that he thought him too dandified, at any rate he ordered Blacky to be saddled. Blacky was a horse that had a habit of kicking out violently the moment anyone called, "Go on, Blacky." After a bit of a struggle Stiller got himself into the saddle. Then someone called "Go

on, Blacky" and Stiller went sailing through the air to the
ruin of his dandified appearance.

He bore this fiasco with equanimity; he even used to tell
the story himself. But his lack of success as script writer was
a different matter. He had not interested any producer in his
ideas. He showed them to Sjöström, who thought them excellent.

"But what do you expect?" Sjöström said to him. "Here
they have their own idea of what is good, that is to say what
the public wants. I and Bergman together made a script of
Ibsen's *The Master Builder* and it was refused. They thought
'that there architect's darned peculiar. If he was so good and
could do such fine plans, why didn't he tell the builder to go
to hell and let a bank finance him? No, "Mr. Seastrom," why
not make a film instead of this story of Elinor Glyn's?' 'But
that's tripe,' I said. 'Elinor Glyn's a famous writer, but who
ever heard of Henrik Ibsen?' was the reply. Then they suggested a book by Hall Caine, and in pure desperation I did
it. I couldn't stand waiting any longer."

When Stiller asked the production people if they had any
suggestions for him, he was given the evasive reply that they
were busy considering a number of things.

Garbo did not feel optimistic either. In the long run, it became difficult to fill her days with just riding and English
lessons. She had been in Hollywood a couple of months now
and had not yet heard a word about a part. It was getting on
her nerves and undermining her self-assurance, which had
never been particularly strong. She became more and more
anxious and in the end felt that all she wanted was not to
have to face a camera.

"I haven't begun work yet," she wrote to a friend, "and

I'm sorry to say that I am not sorry. I don't go to parties, do nothing during the day and just want to go to bed as soon as I can. I'm not smoking so much either, it's this eternally smiling boring sun that takes all one's pleasure away. The doctor told me that the climate here isn't good for me. . . . I don't really know what to think of all the wonders you're told about this place. Just fantasies perhaps. . . . There's no atmosphere at all to the restaurants here and you don't feel you're 'going out' when you dine at one of them. Remember The Opera Cellar!"

Her last film, *Joyless Street*, had had its première and she had been sent the criticisms, which were good as far as she was concerned. "Garbo as usual tall and stately and this time weary for a valid reason." Another paper wrote that she put Asta Neilsen in the shade, but what did the fact of having been relatively successful in two films in a little country like Sweden count in America? She had heard terrifying accounts of the unemployment among actors. In New York alone, 8,000 were without work and in Hollywood 20,000 young girls were going about waiting for a chance, looking for anything. Competition was ruthless.

Now and again she and Stiller went to visiting with some of the Swedish families, where they were regaled with crisp bread, herring and Swedish schnapps. Stiller saw to it that she did not tuck away too much. Why did he want her to starve herself? Before this, he had said nothing about her weight. "But," Stiller insisted, "it was Louis B. Mayer himself who said that you were too fat."

Hm! And here it was Mayer's word that counted. God knows if she would ever get a part at all, even if she waited the full three years.

Mayer had told the production department to see what category they could put the Swedish girl in.

In appearance she was a bit like Theda Bara who had originated the "vamp." Theda was originally a stage actress and had been brought to Hollywood to play a sort of jungle demon in a Kipling picture. She had done well for herself and, for publicity purposes, let it get around that she possessed supernatural powers even in private life.

Garbo had tired eyes and a greedy mouth like Theda. That was the answer—vamp.

No, said Garbo.

What was she then? Surely not a Norma Talmadge, the strict Victorian type, only slightly sentimental?

No!

And not a Clara Bow, with the red hair and Elinor Glyn's *It*?

No!

What sort of part did she see herself in, then?

She wanted to play ordinary people, women who were neither good nor wicked, who could be both proud and humble. She had no desire to play any definite type.

Well, well! They would have to see what they could find.

One day she was told that she was to be driven to the studio for a film test. A make-up man made her up, a hairdresser did her hair and a wardrobe woman garbed her in evening dress. When she saw the result in a mirror, she did not recognize herself. She couldn't possibly do anything dolled up like that. She must speak with Stiller. He wasn't there. They had deliberately omitted to tell him about it.

She had to go through the usual prima donna posturing with slow, sweeping movements and she felt no more alive than a mannequin. The result was bad.

Stiller was furious. He did not rest till he had been allowed to give her another film test himself, the cost of which he paid out of his own pocket. He made her up and combed her, arranged the lights and worked out the camera angles, and, lo and behold, instead of a lifeless chocolate-box beauty, he had created a young woman with a highly individual radiance.

Metro's most successful producer, Irving Thalberg, was to start a new film with Ricardo Cortez in the lead and was looking for a heroine. Thalberg was married to Norma Shearer, but he didn't think the part was good enough for Shearer. When he saw Garbo's first film test, he pronounced her "absolutely unusable," but when he saw what Stiller had done with her he said that she could perhaps be used. Mayer objected that it was too big a part. If Thalberg took her, he must do so on his own responsibility. Thalberg thought that he could make do with her, for he was sure that Cortez' name would make the film a success. And so everything seemed settled. But then something happened that dumfounded two such hard-boiled film makers as Mayer and Thalberg. Greta Garbo did not approve of the part! A twenty-year-old newcomer was going to refuse a job worthy of a star!

The female lead in *The Torrent* was that of a Spanish peasant girl who is loved by the son of the local landowner. He abandons her for a social career and she goes to the capital and in record time becomes a great opera singer, as famous for her voice as for her love affairs. But she is still a country girl at heart and one day she returns to the village with a companion, and wardrobe and jewels which she hasn't earned solely by singing. There is a tremendous thunderstorm and the landowner's son, now a town councilor, hurries to help her. They have an affair and she takes this as a promise of marriage, but when he has had his pleasure with her he abandons her again, and she has to make the trip to America they had planned, alone. Years go by. One fine day she reappears as fresh and youthful as ever, which can't be said of the landowner's son, who has now reached the top of the social ladder but looks like an old man. He pays her a visit in her dressing room. She doesn't recognize him. He now has everything, wealth, honors, power! Everything except. . . . Wouldn't she? No, she certainly won't, for she hasn't got over that business after the thunderstorm. *Finis!*

The only thing not in keeping with the vamp was the fact of her saying "no thank you" to the man's money in the end, but otherwise the part was pure vamp. Monta Bell had been engaged to direct the film, and Stiller was bitterly disappointed that he was not to direct Garbo in her first film in America. He was told that they didn't think the subject suited him. Unselfishly, he advised Garbo to accept the part.

"But it's too silly," Garbo said.

"It can lead to better parts later," Stiller said.

"How can I take direction from someone I don't know? I won't even understand what the man says."

"You can use signs."

The language difficulty was solved by engaging a Swedish actor as interpreter. He was grateful for the money the job brought him and Garbo was happy that she had someone to talk to on the set. Also, a well-known opera singer was engaged to show her how to behave on an opera stage.

Stiller had been refused access to the studio. She felt horribly uncertain and insecure. Cortez treated Garbo like a nobody. To him, she was just an awkward beginner he could scarcely stop patronizing even during their scenes together. He was the great star and considered himself the equal of Valentino—hence the name Ricardo Cortez. His real name was Jacob Krantz. Before this he had had a job with the New York Stock Exchange. His Latin type was less than skin deep and as he was no actor, he was seldom able to convince anyone that he had the eruptive passion of the Latins. When Garbo tried to talk with him, laboriously searching for words, he hardly deigned to reply. An electrician with a sense of humor suggested that she try talking to him in Spanish.

"But I don't know Spanish," Garbo said.

"Neither does he."

She found no support in Monta Bell. Being accustomed to Stiller's severe criticism, she was amazed to find that Bell gave her no individual instructions at all. It was his first film. Before that he had been Chaplin's assistant. His contribution consisted of discovering advantageous scenes and camera angles for Cortez. Garbo sometimes had to act with her back to the camera. She complained to Stiller, who advised her not to make a fuss. A star was a star.

One day they had to get a scene just as the sun went down, at which moment a bomb was to explode. The first take was not successful and as Garbo had got some dirt on her face during the explosion, she left the set for a moment to have her make-up corrected. When Bell called "Clear for second take" and discovered that Garbo was not there, he roared at her interpreter, "Get that big woman back here at once, or I'll miss the sunset!" Garbo, who had heard and understood this, said to the interpreter, "Tell him not to fuss; there'll be plenty more sunsets for him."

When she got back to the studio, she was told that Mayer wished to see her.

What could he want? Had Bell complained? Or did Mayer still think her legs were too fat? She had worn a long dress in all the scenes except one, and then she had been almost hidden by Cortez.

She came into a big room. A receptionist was the only person in sight. As Garbo entered, the woman got to her feet and said ceremoniously, "Miss Garbo?" Then she picked up a telephone and announced her. The door to an adjoining room opened.

Mayer's office would have been suitable for annual general meetings of smaller companies. There he sat, behind a gigantic desk on which was the Metro-Goldwyn-Mayer emblem, the lion and globe. He gestured to a low armchair and she sank so deep that she could not avoid looking up at him. It was like their meeting in Berlin. His head looked as though it grew straight out of his shoulders, and two cold eyes gazed at her from behind black goggles. Her interpreter was also present.

Mayer explained that he had come to the conclusion that three years was too short a time in which to be able to do anything with her as an actress. He wished, therefore, to extend her contract to five years.

With the most innocent expression in the world Garbo replied that she was content with the contract she had.

Mayer looked blank. Had she been warned what he was going to say?

The moment he saw the first takes Mayer realized that Garbo was going to be an attraction. She was like no other great star of the day. This was the time when the girlie type was fashionable and young Americans wanted to resemble flappers, as personified by Clara Bow and Colleen Moore, or the romantic type represented by Janet Gaynor and Lillian Gish. Garbo was something new. Despite her youth, there was a mature sensualism about her which, coupled with a certain haughtiness, greatly increased her sex appeal.

Mayer had her under contract for only three years, of which six months had already passed. The contract must be renewed or extended before the film was shown and she had had time to realize her value. He had consulted Thalberg, who considered that he had made a find in this young Swede. Properly partnered she could become Metro's big star, he told Mayer, and so Mayer had sent for Garbo.

It began to leak out through the technical personnel that the big chiefs had spoken favorably of Garbo after seeing the early scenes of her film. This of course reached Cortez' ears. Now his behavior toward her became definitely impolite.

There was a flooding scene in the film in which the two had to take to the water. Garbo's interpreter stood waiting for her with a couple of warm blankets to wrap around her. Cortez came out first and coolly appropriated both blankets.

"No, Mr. Cortez!" exclaimed the shocked interpreter.

"Let him have them," Garbo said calmly; "you mustn't let yourself be bothered about a pumpkin like that." Pumpkin was her favorite expression for a puffed-up individual.

They had reached one of Garbo's most important scenes, a close-up of the great opera singer accompanying herself on a piano. Garbo struck a chord and jumped. It was a real piano, not a dummy. During the take she carefully pretended to play and, in order to hide her ignorance of what she was do-ing, sang a Swedish song she knew, with much feeling. Monta Bell pricked up his ears. "My God," he said, "what a voice and what expression. If only we could use it!"

A week later Mayer asked Garbo to come and see him again. This time he began by lamenting that it had taken so long to get her started working. She must remember that all this time he had not only been paying her full salary, but had spent money on publicity for her. As time went on this expenditure would grow and grow. If Metro was to have any chance of recovering even part of its outlay, her contract must be extended for at least another two years.

That meant five years. Garbo had never contemplated being away for so long. In fact, three years was quite long enough in a foreign country.

Mayer removed his goggles and looked at her. Was she simple or was she being cute?

"You see, Miss Garbo," he said, "some people make a hit and some are flops in this movie business. If you stay long enough with us, I think I could make a hit of you. I don't know why, but somehow I feel it here." He laid his hand on his heart and looked emotional.

Calmly, Garbo gathered up her gloves and bag and said, "Nevertheless, I want to go home."

Mayer got up and looked like an advocate preparing to make a last appeal on behalf of a client who has said something stupid.

Was it really her intention to put obstacles in her own way and go back to Sweden? He looked as though he were about to cry. "Miss Garbo, believe me, when you're sitting there at home eating your herring and potato, you will regret it when you think that you could have stayed here and lived on chicken and champagne."

As often as Garbo had time and energy (filming was a great strain on her strength and nerves) she went to see Stiller. She was depressed by her performance. Stiller had not seen any of the takes, but he did his best to console her.

Stiller had disregarded friends' warnings and gone out thinly clad after the raw mists had drifted in from the sea. He had got it into his head that he must harden himself, but instead he had contracted severe rheumatism. Garbo fussed over him with rugs and hot drinks.

It was the end of November. Garbo, too, was amazed to find how cold it could be in California. She mentioned this in a letter home and a few weeks later received a parcel containing a pair of mittens her sister Alva had knitted and a tin of her mother's gingerbread. Greta was touched. Christmas was approaching and her letter of acknowledgment was filled with homesickness.

> It almost makes me ill when I think that I can't come home and spend Christmas with you, have a spruce, *lutfisk* and nuts. Can't go out and feel that wonderful Christmas atmosphere, no popping in and out of the shops in Drottningsgatan and Regeringsgatan laden with parcels. I suppose I'm stupid and ungrateful, when you consider that perhaps there are millions whose dearest wish is to be in my shoes. But there it is. Mauritz is not too well. . . .

But one day Mauritz was better—at least in a better mood. In a bookshop he had come across some German translations of recent novels, including one by the Spanish writer Blasco-Ibañez, *La terra de todos*. As they ate, he told Garbo the plot.

"What do you think of that Helen of Troy figure, the Marquesa de Torrebianca?" he asked.

"All right."

"Would you like to play her?"

Garbo nodded. She thought the part a bit too speculative, perhaps, but there was a good denouement and also it was important that Mauritz should have something to occupy him.

As usual, when he had a new idea, Stiller announced that this was going to be his best film. In two weeks he had a synopsis ready, and this time he got the chiefs—at least

Mayer and Thalberg—to listen to him, not because they thought what he had written particularly good, but because in their eyes Ibañez was a good author now that one of his books had been a successful serial in the Hearst magazines.

But there was a lot that had to be changed. The female part was far too predominant. How would you get a star to play the male lead, if his role wasn't of at least equal importance?

The male part couldn't possibly be equal, Stiller objected, because the woman's part was the whole basis of the action.

Also, they went on without listening to him, the world's full of squeamish people. They are our public and they don't want to feel as though they have had a grilling when they go home. The least they ask in return for their money is a good time, otherwise they won't go.

Shakespeare, Stiller retorted, had drawn full houses for four hundred years and no one can say that he was afraid of upsetting people.

Well, Shakespeare was all right, no doubt, but he couldn't write films. "Film isn't drama, Mr. Stiller, it's mathematics; so and so many feet of love, so and so many feet of humor, so and so many feet of scenery. Believe me!" Mayer said.

Stiller attempted a compromise. If it were essential to make changes in his story, he wanted to make them himself.

"Mr. Stiller"—Mayer took the cigar from his mouth, to emphasize his words—"the biggest best seller ever—the Bible—was written by a whole corporation."

Although, like Stiller, Mayer had been born in Russia of Jewish parents, the two men just didn't speak the same language. He had started as Ludwig Metzer, scrap dealer, and advanced to proprietor of a small movie house, where he himself turned the handle of the projector. So when he came to Hollywood to stake his money, he was very much the self-made man. He had even made his own name, changing Ludwig Metzer to Louis B. Mayer.

And he changed more than that. The little Jewish boy from Minsk became more American than any American. The Stars and Stripes hung in his office and his slogan was "Films for the American Family." He had nothing against sex, he said, but it must be honest American sex and not unseemly. Amongst the unseemly he included directors with their own, newfangled ideas, since their films showed a tendency to cost too much. Such people had to be softened up and made willing to cooperate. Mayer wanted as good a return as possible from his capital; films were a business for him, while for Stiller they were art.

The very mention of the word "art" made Mayer see red. "You say you want to make art, Mr. Stiller. Who is to pay for it—you yourself? The public won't. We can't. We haven't that much money. We make the films that people want."

Stiller groaned. His script went to the script department for treatment.

The Torrent had its world première in Loew's State Theater in Los Angeles and the Capitol in New York. The next morning, Garbo could say with Lord Byron, "I woke and found myself famous." Everyone was talking about her. On Broadway a queue of people four abreast circled the corner of Fifty-first Street. The press thought her a combination of Pola Negri, Alma Rubens and Norma Talmadge. Her likeness to Talmadge was especially striking. But they also thought that in more than one respect Garbo was heads above the other three. The other principals were not as fortunate; Monta Bell's unimaginative direction and the silly script were soundly criticized. Cortez, the star, was quite put in the shade and it was no use emphasizing in interviews that Garbo was merely his leading lady. The questions they asked him were about her, and he found it difficult to attract attention.

Garbo did not lose her head. She wrote home:

> My first film is now on at the Capitol, the biggest movie theater in New York, for a second week, which people here regard as unprecedented, and they say it is because of me. . . . The public and critics have been wonderfully kind, but personally I don't think I was good, so I can't get much pleasure out of that. They don't have a type like me out here, so if I can't learn to act, they'll soon tire of me, I expect.

She had no need to wait for her next part. *The Temptress* was already on the production list.

Stiller had had his script back, furnished with Ibañez' own name, at a great cost to Metro, and altered beyond recognition. Of the main figure, with her finely differentiated character, there remained only a highly sexed demon who gobbled men up one after the other. Garbo found the part even more repugnant than her role in *The Torrent*, but it was Stiller's chance and so she made it a condition of acceptance that he should direct it. After her success in *The Torrent* they were beginning to heed her wishes.

It wasn't easy for Stiller to arouse enthusiasm either in himself or Garbo for this now thoroughly banal story of a young woman brought up in the most frivolous circles in Paris, who, before finding her "great love," manages to ruin a succession of men, driving them out of their heads—to suicide or letting them kill each other in gory duels. The hero and a villain fight an Argentine duel with long whips, torsos bare, blindfolded.

For the male lead it was necessary to find an actor who

was not merely a dressed-up doll. A puppet would just have emphasized the outlandish character of the plot. And Garbo's partner had to be fairly tall. This was a problem since, like the women, the male stars were all very short: Colman, Valentino, Richard Barthelmess, Ramon Novarro, were all under average height.

Metro suggested Antonio Moreno.

"He's too short," Stiller said.

"Or is Garbo, perhaps, too tall?" was the retort.

"He's a bad actor," Stiller said.

"But you're an eminent director. It will be your business to take him in hand. With his Latin origin, Moreno ought to make an excellent South American," they told him.

For some reason Stiller did not know, it had been decided from the beginning that Moreno was to play the part and it only remained for him to make the best of a bad job.

Moreno was conceited and looked like a gigolo. Stiller said that he must shave off his mustache.

"Why?" Moreno asked.

"Because you look like an Italian waiter."

Moreno was furious. He went to the chiefs and demanded that Stiller apologize.

"Why should I?" said Stiller. "He does look like an Italian waiter."

Stiller did not realize what an influential person he was insulting. Moreno had married money and had a financial interest in Metro. He himself decided what parts he should have.

Filming began without Stiller apologizing or Moreno shaving his mustache. Both looked daggers at each other.

On the fourth day they were taking a full-length shot of the two lovers on a sofa. Stiller went up to Moreno and asked him to put on a pair of larger shoes in order to make Garbo's feet look smaller. This was too much for Moreno; he left the studio and refused to do any more work on the film as long as Stiller was directing it.

While the Metro chiefs discussed what was to be done, they continued filming the scenes that did not require Moreno's presence. Stiller now had to accept the control of a couple of "supervisors" who continually altered his directions. He was not accustomed to that and had to be told that here he was merely a cog in a wheel that others set in motion. There were violent scenes between him and the Metro front office.

"They engage me because they think I have good ideas about how films should be made," he complained to Sjöström, "and then I'm not allowed to do anything without the busybodies interfering everywhere."

Sjöström tried to mediate. He got himself and Stiller invited to the home of an influential director who was also head of the studios. Cautiously, circumspectly, Sjöström tried to point out that the final result would be best where the director of a film had the sole responsibility for it. A film ought to be a one-man job; but he could not convince the other nor effect an understanding between the sober-minded Metro businessman and Stiller with his heated artistic imagination.

As the two were leaving the house, built like a miniature Grecian temple, the indignant Stiller thumped his fist on one of the pillars at the entrance. It rang hollow.

"Listen," he said, "it isn't called Hollow-wood for nothing."

Filming continued in an oppressive atmosphere and without Moreno. When Stiller became excited all his English save two words deserted him. When he disapproved of someone

he would point at the culprit exclaiming, "Hallo, hallo!" and
then with a violent shake of the head, "No, no!" The actors, including Lionel Barrymore and Roy d'Arcy, considered him a figure of fun.

In a restaurant scene, a moment arose when the other actors were supposed to applaud, and Stiller had had the word
drummed into him so that he could properly instruct the
actors. After the rehearsals and the first take, one of the supervisors objected to a number of things, and at the retake Stiller
was so distraught that instead of "Applaud," he shouted
"Explode"—which everyone did!

As Moreno still refused to resume work, Stiller received a
note saying that as of the next day he must consider himself
relieved of the direction of the film. It was a great blow, not
only for him, but also for Garbo. Together they went to see
Victor Sjöström, who said afterward that Stiller was so despondent that he wept. Garbo was touching in her endeavor
to comfort him. "You mustn't worry about this, Mauritz,
you know that you're the best director there is. It doesn't
matter what they think."

Fred Niblo was brought in to finish the film. It was he
who had made *Ben Hur* the previous year, the company's
most expensive picture at that time, costing more than a million dollars (in 1925!). Niblo was a specialist in mass scenes
and not accustomed to instructing individuals. He admired
Garbo and told Mayer, "There's nothing so difficult as to
arouse sympathy in an unattractive part, but Garbo can."
Yet his attempts to achieve contact with her were fruitless.
He paid for the dress designer Garbo preferred out of his
own pocket, but when he asked her if she was happy now, she
didn't look a bit happier.

She suffered on Stiller's account and wrote in a letter,

"Why should things always be so difficult for Mauritz? He is one of the best directors there is. You know, I could have cried when I saw the opposition growing up round him and how it became more and more difficult for him to concentrate. I hope that at least it will be possible to fix something for him. . . ."

Stiller himself made no mention of the occurrence. In a letter to a friend, he merely hints that he is not happy. "I would like best just to take my money and go home, but my contract's for three years. But then you'll see . . . Garbo's filming with Niblo who's a fine director. If she can just endure it, she can earn millions here. . . ."

There now followed a very difficult time for Garbo. Filming lasted from seven in the morning till six in the evening, and after that she usually had to arrange her costumes. "I loathe clothes," she said. "I have never been interested in them, and all these fittings and discussions with tailors and seamstresses take the stuffing out of me. When eventually I get to bed, I'm so tired that often I can't sleep. Then I lie thinking about that business with Mauritz."

When news came from home that her sister Alva had died, Garbo felt as though she wouldn't be able to carry on. Niblo wanted to redo all the parts of the film that Stiller had made and it looked as though production would never end.

"I've been on my second film for five months now," she wrote. "You have no idea how hard one has to work here, it's beyond one's strength. I have asked for permission to come home, but of course it would be mad after making only one film . . . since Mauritz went there's no one to look after me, I feel lonely and abandoned. . . ."

One day, on the way to her dressing room, she met a face that smiled to her through its heavy layers of paint. It was

Lon Chaney, the man of a thousand faces. He was another
who preferred to keep out of the social whirl. Despite the
language difficulty, he understood Garbo and she liked him,
because there was nothing swell-headed about him, as so
often was the case with the others, nor did he use the dreadful jargon of film circles.

"How are you, Garbo girl?" was his greeting when they
shared a table for lunch. His advice to her was, "Don't let anyone influence you; just be yourself." Sometimes, when she
was so depressed that she rested in her dressing room instead
of having lunch, Chaney went to Borg, her interpreter, to ask
how she was and added, "Tell her not to worry."

One day Chaney wanted to show Garbo the set where his
own film was being made. In this picture he played a blind
man and Garbo watched as, before going on, he sprayed his
eyeballs with a thick gray fluid to look blind. "But Lon," she
exclaimed, "is that really necessary? Suppose it damaged
your eyesight."

"I don't think it will," he replied, smiling. "One must do
something for the dough."

When she got back, she asked her interpreter what
"dough" was. "Money," he told her. She nodded thought-
fully. "Lon's right. There's a lot one has to do for one's
money."

On one of the last filming days, the Crown Prince and Princess of Sweden visited Hollywood.

"You know that the Crown Prince and Princess Louise
were here," Garbo wrote. "Lunch in the Metro-Goldwyn
studio. With Miss Garbo on Gustaf Adolf's right! I was a
quarter of an hour late—scandal! He was very nice but I
pulled several boners and offered him cigarettes, though
everyone knows that he neither smokes nor drinks. Why does

one always do things one doesn't intend? One always does something silly . . . I am so tired; I never go out, just collapse into bed. Oh God, to be able to go home, when the time's up. If I have a bit of money by then, it would be fine. But no increase in my salary yet—they are mean!"

After six months *The Temptress* was finished at last.

In order to get the reaction of the average movie-goer and to avoid showing it to a mere crowd of film people, the Metro directors had decided to hold the preview in a theater out in Santa Monica. The news leaked out, however, and as people were very curious to see the Swedish star's second film, when Stiller and Garbo got there the audience seemed to consist almost exclusively of film people. Garbo became nervous. The atmosphere, at first expectant, became chillier and chillier as the film progressed. Stiller muttered and shifted in his seat. The Sjöströms were there and hurried out as soon as it was over, in order to avoid expressing an opinion. Ghastly, was the general verdict.

Out in the hall amidst a cluster of Metro people Stiller gave vent to his wrath in German: *"Es ist ein Skandal!"*

Another Scandinavian couple, named Gade, were searching for their car outside, when they saw to their horror that Stiller and Garbo were coming toward them. There was no need for them to say anything, however, for Stiller shouted to them from a distance: "That was rotten—dreadful. We must have something to drink, but I haven't a drop at home. Let's go to your place instead."

Gade had thought that in the film Garbo had been neither beautiful nor interesting, though in real life she was both; and, worst of all, quite without talent. But he felt so sorry for her that he praised something she had done as he was helping her off with her coat in the hall.

"Oh, no! I'm ashamed," she said and fled into the sitting room, where Stiller was gulping down a large whisky.

"What a damned mess," he began, banging his great fist on the table and making the glasses jump. "Here I've discovered the girl, taken the risk of giving her the lead in *Gösta Berling* and succeeded in making her known wherever films are shown, and then these bunglers come and ruin everything I've done."

Gade tried to soothe him. It surely wasn't quite as bad as that. If certain scenes were redone and various other bits pruned, it might make quite a decent film. But Stiller went on, now addressing Garbo.

"How the devil could you spend six months acting that without feeling how dreadful you were?" Garbo looked around in despair. "And the way your hair was done! You could at least have made yourself up properly; as it was you looked like—I won't say what!"

Garbo began to cry.

Then Mrs. Gade came in with some champagne, just at the right moment.

"Now we'll forget about *The Temptress* and drink to Garbo's future."

Garbo shook her head.

"Greta," Gade said, "you know perfectly well that in Europe you can get as many and whatever parts you like, in spite of this."

They drank and Garbo's tears mingled with the champagne. She was utterly despondent about the future.

Stiller tried to get the film stopped. Were they really going to throw away an asset like Garbo by showing that ghastly stuff?

Nonsense, said Mayer. Anyway the film was already distributed to all parts of America.

The première took place in New York the following week, again at the Capitol. It was an even greater success than *The Torrent*. The newspapers showered Garbo with praise. As with her first film, the praise was entirely for Garbo. Because of the film's great success, the management of the Capitol gave a special Swedish night. Everyone thought Garbo was magnificent.

Before the première in Sweden, she wrote a friend, "I must ask you all in advance to forgive *The Temptress*. There's nothing good in it. The script and direction couldn't be worse and I myself am beneath criticism. But I was so down all the time, and besides I'm coming to realize more and more that I'm really no actress. . . ."

By that she meant that she couldn't change herself, and that she wasn't like the dreadful women they kept demanding her to play. If she didn't feel she had earned any laurels to put on her tired brow, at least it was pleasant to have finished the filming which had proved such a strain on her nerves. Now she could breathe again and feel human.

Chapter 11

JOHN GILBERT

But the Metro people were not ones to let the grass grow under their feet. They wanted to produce a whole series of films with this new discovery of theirs.

A week after the première they sent her a new script, *The Flesh and the Devil*, based on a novel by Hermann Sudermann. What was the idea? Was she to start work again so soon?

She read the script and writhed. Again a demimonde. Almost hysterical at the thought of having to play another slut, she went in person to see Mayer. He must let her off! She was tired and depressed and needed time to recover. Couldn't she rest for a few weeks at least and then come back with new strength—and to a different part?

"Nonsense," Mayer said. "You're to begin next week. Your clothes are ready for fitting."

Then something unheard of happened.

Garbo did not turn up for her fittings. She never even appeared in the studio. At her hotel she was not available. Mayer wrote, threatening to withhold her salary. He sent for her interpreter, Borg, and told him, "You can tell that scullery maid to go back where she comes from."

They begged and pleaded, but Garbo did not emerge from her hiding place. They looked for her everywhere. She had vanished.

The person who discovered her whereabouts proved to be a fellow named Harry Edington, a well-known Hollywood manager. He succeeded in getting to see her and told her that the film was to be directed by Clarence Brown, whom Edington had under personal contract. She, of course, had seen the Valentino film that Brown had made, *The Eagle*. But above all, Brown was known as the director of all Norma Talmadge's films; he was the special star-maker with proven ability in promoting a star's interests, which was why Talmadge had been able to last so long.

Garbo nodded absently while Edington talked.

But it wasn't only Clarence Brown. Edington was also impresario for the male lead, John Gilbert, and so had a dual interest in getting the film started, provided Garbo took on the female lead. If she would, the film was a success before it was even made.

Garbo laughed. Clever fellow that Edington.

Three days later she was in the studio.

Clarence Brown has told how he introduced Garbo and Gilbert to each other. "It was love at first sight, and it lasted a long time. In front of the camera their love-making was so intense that it surpassed anything anyone had seen and made the technical staff feel their mere presence an indiscretion. Sometimes they did not even hear my 'cut,' but went on, to the cameraman's amusement."

Garbo, who usually sat by herself in a corner between takes, now amazed the whole studio by starting to chat and laugh, and Gilbert was all fire as he watched the mysterious, desirable Greta.

Behind his swarthy exterior with darting eyes and dazzling smile, Gilbert was truly masculine, immoderate and unbalanced, a man who liked to keep late hours, preferably with a beautiful woman. He was a big, wild lad who considered it his duty in private life to live up to his reputation as the movies' greatest lover. Thus, whenever he got a new leading lady, he was in a hurry to press her to his masculine chest. He liked handling firearms and always had a loaded revolver lying on his bedside table. He used to say quite seriously that he would empty it into the first rival who ventured into his bedroom to disturb his sleep.

He asked Garbo to marry him and did up a large house for them both—even before he obtained her assent. Proudly he showed her the bathroom, all white tile.

"How horribly shiny!" said Garbo. Immediately he had them changed to black. "Oh, John, you're such a child!" was Garbo's only comment.

They were being talked and whispered about everywhere. They had been seen in a car together; they were supposed to have bathed together; they had been walking here and there and everywhere. Journalists with cameras crouched behind every bush, but they never got their pictures, and some were forced to invent gossip in order to avoid being fired for their failure to provide material. It was always possible to enlarge on the theme of tiny Gilbert versus the giant Stiller, who in press circles went by the name of Mount Everest. Stiller-Garbo, "the most unusual looking couple in filmdom," were seldom seen now, for the place of Mount Everest had been taken by "divine Jack." One day, they were reported as engaged, the next as good as married.

A New York newspaper stated:

> The Romeo of the films who wasn't going to marry again now engaged to Swedish actress. Handsome, dashing Jack Gilbert is defeated. Hollywood is on tenterhooks. His heart is riddled, he has begun to like things Swedish. Jack began to show signs of restlessness several months ago when his film work brought him into passionate contact with that desirable feminine gift from Sweden—Greta Garbo. Jack showed his love for Greta so openly that rumor began to spread its wings, and Greta returned it so openly that rumor took flight. Now comes the news that Jack is to marry Greta. What a couple! Both have been fashioned in the fire of love. Both are temperamental, stormy, beautiful.

Even the children in school talked about it, and when the Sjöströms' two girls came home one day and found Aunt Greta there, they asked, "Do you like Jack?"

"Yes, Jack's nice," Garbo said.

"Are you going to marry him?"

Garbo laughed.

Gilbert was a scatterbrain where money was concerned, and Greta soon had an example of this when he bought a luxury yacht, called it *The Temptress*, and fitted it out in accordance with what he imagined was her taste.

Conrad Nagel has related how he, the Thalbergs and King Vidor were invited aboard one Sunday and received by Gilbert in well-fitting yachting attire. They were shown around and had all the refinements of *The Temptress* pointed out to them.

"But," said Norma Shearer, "we thought we caught a

glimpse of Garbo as we came aboard; where's she gone to?"

Gilbert smiled slyly. Garbo was hiding in the crew's quarters.

According to a member of the crew, the couple never went out that day after all, for when it came time to raise anchor, Garbo went home in her car.

A week later *The Temptress* changed hands. There were many other examples of Garbo's irresolution in her association with Gilbert. When Gilbert had been drinking—and he drank most of the time—he often ran wild, either in a car or on foot.

One evening, Garbo locked herself in her suite in Gilbert's house and refused to join the party he had arranged. He kept banging on her door, more and more violently each time.

"Open the door!"

"No. I want to sleep. Go away now, like a good boy."

Angrily Gilbert rushed to his garage, got into his car, and disappeared with a furious blast of his horn. His wild career was halted in Wilshire Boulevard and he spent the night in the lockup, where he was a frequent guest.

Garbo had made their relationship pretty clear in a letter.

> No doubt, like everybody else, you have heard about me and a certain actor, but we are not going to be married. When I come home we shall have our bachelor evenings— for bachelor I intend to remain. I wouldn't make a wife.

But the press persisted. One newspaper reported that she and Gilbert had gone to Santa Ana one night to get married, but that when they were before the justice of the peace, the brutal Stiller had come bursting in and stopped the proceedings. "He could have crushed them both in one hand. But what use is brute strength?" the paper added philosophi-

Garbo at seventeen.

Dull's Presstjänst

The 1924 class at the Royal Dramatic School, Stockholm. Garbo is on the extreme right and Mimi Pollack is next to her.

Dull's Presstjänst

Garbo in her favorite role of harem girl and Mimi Pollack as a South Sea beauty at a fancy-dress ball in Stockholm.

Garbo, wearing a white blouse, in one of her earliest motion picture appearances, a commercial film advertising the products of a Stockholm bakery.

Dull's Presstjänst

A bathing beauty in her first full-length film, Garbo is standing with her arms stretched. Petschler is standing next to the camera.

hough still an un-
own, Garbo was
n her first starring
in *Gösta Berling*,
novie made from
ma Lagerlöf's
dish classic by the
iant impresario
ritz Stiller.

Dull's Presstjänst

Dull's Presstjänst

Filming a scene from *Gösta Berling*. Lars Hanson, the hero, is sitting on Garbo's right and Stiller is standing beside the camera.

Here Garbo is at a railway station in Bulgaria on a filming trip to Turkey. This early Stiller project ended disastrously.

Brown Brothers

A scene from *The Temptress*, 1926. *From left to right*: Stiller, Garbo, Lon Chaney, Fred Niblo, Antonio Moreno.

Garbo with her director, Sjöström, during the filming of A *Divine Woman*, 1928.

Garbo arrived in the United States with Stiller in 1925 on the Swedish ship *Drottningholm*.

Brown Brothers

Garbo's first American home.

Dull's Presstjänst

At first the publicity men wanted to make Garbo the rugged sports girl.

Dull's Presstjänst

Garbo (*second from the left*) as Anna Karenina, 1927.

A well-known pose from *Anna Christie*, 1930.

With Nils Asther in *Wild Orchids,* 1929.

With John Gilbert outside the studio.

Garbo and four of her most romantic male leads.

With Lew Ayres in *The Kiss,* 1929.

With Clark Gable in *Susan Lenox,* 1930.

Mother and daughter c
brate a warm reunion.

Dull's Presstjänst

*Back to Sweden for th
time.*

Also there is the renewa
the old friendship v
Mimi Pollack (*seated
car.*)

Dull's Presstjänst

Garbo in *Queen Chris-tina*, 1933.

Disembarking from the *Ile de France* in New York, 1949.

With Robert Taylor in *Camille*, 1937.

Landing at Orly Field, 1951. Garbo's companion is Mrs. John Gunther.

Brown Brothers

A rare picture of Garbo standing on the corner of 57th Street and Madison Avenue, 1952.

Brown Brothers

Garbo (*right*) vacationing on
Capri, 1955.

Brown Brothers

Wearing the ine~~
dark glasses,
brushes by reporter
arriving at Orly
1956.

Brown Brothers

cally. "Jack's wooing was so different from Stiller's. Jack is a volcano married to a hurricane. Stiller is a slow-moving giant who could crush Greta with one hand. But her heart escapes his physical prowess and this she has given to Mr. Gilbert."

Afterward, when there was neither a baby nor a wedding, the papers had to invent an excuse, so that their readers would not feel duped. Garbo was cold and hard, too much the descendant of the Vikings for the fragile Gilbert, who had not been able to stand so much cold in the long run.

In other words, there was no doubt who had thrown over whom. For what girl could get out of John's clutches once he had got his hands on her? Leatrice Joy, Virginia Bruce, and Mary Hay were some of the many. Before this business with Garbo he had been engaged to a young author in Metro's script department, Dorothy Parker. His thirst for victims seemed endless, and when he was forced to give Garbo up, he literally flung himself at Beatrice Lillie.

Garbo herself has said that she could never have managed her third American film without Gilbert. He made her forget how much she disliked both her part and the whole film. *The Flesh and the Devil* was a typical triangle drama. Gilbert's rival for Garbo was none other than Lars Hanson, who had played in *Gösta Berling*. He had been lured over by the Hollywood salaries and had also taken his doctor's advice to rest his voice awhile.

Hanson thought Gilbert a fine fellow but too conscious of his position as star. "One day," he said, "when I was in fine form and had really got going, Gilbert went to Brown and told him that he must curb me a bit. He wanted to dominate."

The advance interest in the film was enormous. The audience at the preview in Hollywood was a gala show in itself, and crowds had gathered to see the famous screen stars at close view.

There was Eric von Stroheim looking exactly as in his films, an unhappy bull; Basil Rathbone and his wife; Clara Bow and the exotic Mexican beauty, Lupe Velez, with escorts who had just "arrived." One looked muscular, with a low forehead and eyebrows that joined together; he used to be an extra and had made himself the he-man of he-men, Clark Gable. The other was tall, with a cowboy's awkwardness and the winning smile of a schoolboy, Gary Cooper. Tallulah Bankhead, frivolous and charming, came alone. Always the original, greeting people with a hoarse "hello." Then Emil Jannings walking like a sailor and talking in an unexpectedly high voice and heavy accent. With him was his wife and pretty, grown-up daughter. Then Joan Crawford, a night-club dancer who had just kicked her way onto the screen, escorted by Douglas Fairbanks, Jr. Behind them his father, Douglas, with huge white teeth in a vast expanse of sunburn, with Mary Pickford, permanently "fourteen years old."

Next came Adolphe Menjou, who made his first big success in Chaplin's *A Woman of Paris*. With him was a sweet young thing who could have been his daughter and was his wife. Then Hollywood's most confirmed bachelor, Ronald Colman; and the lovely Gloria, with the Marquis de Falaise and only three of her nine lap dogs, the white turban and white dress on the girlish figure that contrasted with her blasé features. Buster Keaton, the man who never smiled, followed them. And that woman with the half-shut eyes and sensual mouth, was that Garbo? No, Pola Negri with the great director Lubitsch and his big cigar.

Garbo and Gilbert stayed away.

Garbo wrote home, "In a couple of days my third American film with John Gilbert and Lars Hanson will have its première. But I shan't go to the gala opening if I can avoid it. I'll slip in the next evening if I'm all right."

The greatest sensation of the picture was the fact that Garbo had been daring enough to kiss with open mouth. All tickets for the première in New York were sold weeks in advance. Everyone wanted to see this new pair of lovers and the film broke all records on Broadway. One cay say that *The Flesh and the Devil* was what really established Garbo, because in Europe the critics had been fairly reserved about her two previous films, and in Sweden they had used the word "fiasco." Now, however, the Swedes were proud of her indeed. "It is a pity that Strindberg is no longer alive," one critic remarked, "for he would have recognized and applauded her satanic Felicitas who throws over and betrays her lover in order to live in luxury and ease. The film could just as well have been called 'The Dance of Death.'" Clarence Brown's direction was praised. Gilbert and Hanson were excellent, but it was Garbo's film. There was nothing but praise.

Garbo's mother was interviewed in Blekinge Street. Did she hear from Greta nowadays?

"Oh yes, Greta is sweet and kind and writes so often."

"What does she say?"

"Well, in her last letter she said that I was to tell everyone at home that it isn't at all as they imagine out there. We haven't the time to live lives of revelry, she said. When we get off, we're happy to be able to go home and to bed. Oh, yes, I thought her good, of course. Though they didn't need to kiss so much."

The Flesh and the Devil made Garbo's name known all over the world. Everyone wanted to meet her: fellow actors, film fans, celebrities, and royalty; but she was exhausted and wanted to be left in peace. She isolated herself, with the result that people's curiosity about her became all the more intense. When she appeared, people sometimes came right up and tried to touch her. She became scared and refused to see anyone.

Prince Wilhelm of Sweden was in Hollywood and Metro wanted to arrange a meeting. Garbo refused. It would just be the usual battery of cameras and hundreds of eyes peering at her. Metro tried again, emphasizing that this was a royal personage from her own country and they wanted to give a big lunch in his honor.

"Thank you," she replied, "but I'm not hungry."

Reporters besieged her to get an interview with "the Swedish charmer." She wouldn't give interviews. They wrote them all the same, some sensible, some so silly they might have been meant for comic papers. Here is an example of the latter kind:

THE VIKING'S CONQUEST

Such was the caption. Then followed a description of her appearance:

> Her face cannot be described. No one could believe that such devilish beauty existed in this world. Her eyes are blue—childishly blue one moment, hellishly black the next. Her forehead is high and white. One moment it radiates the purity of all pure women; the next moment it is disfigured by the lusts of the whole world. On her mouth is now the innocent smile of a child, now it is twisted to something mortally horrible—a meeting place for all the blazing passion and profligate sensualism that has been since earth was created. What an astounding enigma this woman is, what a mystery, what an unhappy, complicated soul.

Then followed the interview.

She is lying on a rose-colored sofa with her inevitable cigarette. It is lunchtime, but she isn't eating.

"I can't sleep in this country. I don't know why," she says. She speaks with a drawl and a marked foreign accent. [The woman reporter remarks that she thought the Vikings' daughter was in love, because she could not sleep. But, she goes on,] I soon discovered that she wasn't and never had been. Greta Garbo is awake, but not roused. She has flashed across the American firmament. The strife and lawless love of a thousand years flows in her veins. A thousand forgotten years ago a red-haired, golden-bearded, carefree freebooter stepped aboard his little ship in a Swedish fjord and sailed forth on his successful, daring Viking voyage—a little craft setting out to conquer the world! A thousand dreamless years passed and then Greta Garbo arrived—in all her immaculate beauty—into this beauty-hungry world. And in that same Swedish fjord one day last year a young talented girl stepped aboard a big ocean liner to voyage forth and CONQUER THE WORLD. But it is a cruel thing, an atrocious thing to create anything so beautiful, so devilishly well equipped as Greta Garbo. It happens only once in an eternity and in such a creature's tracks there inevitably follow unhappiness, tragedy and despair. For, despite her golden-blonde inheritance, Greta Garbo is an unhappy woman, a tragic artist. She doesn't understand that men can become mad about her or women bow in admiration. She does not see that directors, actors and the public lie at her feet.

"What do you do to amuse yourself in your spare time?"
She sighs and answers, "Nothing."
"Do you play golf?"
"No."
"But what do you do?"
"Nothing. Just work." Another sigh. Then she wakes to life. "I should prefer to be dead than to love, and I would rather be dead than not to love. Love comes, love goes. Who can help it?" Lots of sighs. A fresh cigarette. She doesn't

seem to have any more to say, but leans back heavily, so young, so weary, so tragically, earthily beautiful. I haven't the heart to bother her with more questions. I let her alone, sighing, unhappy, enigmatic, unsatisfied—as she is doomed to remain.

There were others who, when refused an interview, reacted with silence, an ominous silence while they bided their time, awaiting their chance. They had no need to wait long.

It leaked out that the conflict between Garbo and Metro was becoming more serious. The newspapers began to write that success had gone to the young Swedish girl's head. She was not only dissatisfied with her salary, but wanted to decide what parts she was to play. Garbo, the incarnation of sophistication, now wanted to play "sweet roles" and for that, according to her chief, Mr. Mayer, she was no more qualified than Gloria Swanson.

"If I had granted her wishes in that direction," he has said, "her film career would have ended there."

Garbo's reply to that would have been that she had no desire to be an arch-Cleopatra, and that she had had enough of vamping and playing the slattern.

The company asked how anyone could call her new part that of a slattern? The script was based on real literature, Tolstoi's *Anna Karenina*. The author's own son had been engaged to guarantee the genuineness of the film and Dmitri Buchowetzky, a Russian, was to direct it, and the film title was *Love*.

Despite praiseworthy ambitions the planning of the film was debatable in several respects. The casting was not the most suitable: Lionel Barrymore was to be Karenin; Ricardo Cortez the lover, Vronsky. Garbo maintained that, as usual, her own part had been distorted and stereotyped, a criticism that later was to prove perfectly justified.

The quarrel persisted. Even in Sweden she was accused of putting on prima donna's airs and of not being intelligent enough to stand success. But her letters home show that she was anxious, worried, afraid of falling out with her employer, yet feeling that she must fight in order to avoid parts for which she did not feel suited:

> Things have been happening here since I last wrote, I can tell you. I get so nervous from playing these parts that I quite lose my head. When they came and wanted me to do *The Flesh and the Devil* I simply stayed at home. That was a great scandal. In the end I was forced to play it. After that they had the effrontery to give me an even worse part and Buchowetzky as my director. Then I went a second time. Now I'm considered mad, and I've heard that they're thinking of having my passport stopped. I'm worried how it's all going to turn out. . . . Mauritz has made a film with Pola Negri, which everyone considers excellent, truly European and so full of atmosphere. It has brought him a contract with Paramount. I really do hope that he, who hasn't had so much friendliness shown him at home, will become one of the leading directors here, if not the leading one.

Stiller had put into effect his plan of getting into contact with his old friend Pommer at Paramount and had his script *Hotel Stadt Lemberg* accepted. The only thing that was changed was the title; Lemberg had a German sound. It was too soon after the first World War. The name was changed to *Hotel Imperial.*

After the fiasco with Metro, Stiller felt that his artistic reputation in America would stand or fall with the film. He toiled at it like a galley slave, sitting up at night to prepare the next day's takes. The result was superb.

The preview was a great success, Garbo wrote. "It was wonderful to see Mauritz being paid homage by those who previously had disregarded him. He was bursting with happiness. I just squeezed his hand, for I knew that if I had said anything, he would have burst into tears."

But Stiller and America just did not go together. After making half of a film with Emil Jannings as a Salvation Army man, he fell out with the Paramount chiefs when they wanted him to redo a number of the scenes. After that Stiller had had enough of America and decided to go back to Sweden.

Garbo had just spent her third Christmas in Hollywood. Letters from home brought her news of frost and snow in Stockholm. The young people were skiing and skating. She could picture the scene and the royal palace in its wintry garb. The New Year was in the offing . . . a new year in Hollywood.

The struggle with Metro continued. Both sides were waiting for the other to give in. Metro asked the authorities not to prolong her permission to work; Garbo replied that she had already packed and had no greater wish than to be able to go home. One person, wise in the ways of the world, who advised her most definitely not to go was Emil Jannings, whom she had got to know through Stiller.

"Believe me, Greta," he said to her, "no one lasts long in this profession. In five or six years another comes and takes your place. Stay where you are and work as long as you can. You have no reason to go, when the public wants to see you."

Then she received a second visit from Harry Edington, who now offered to act as her agent. Wanting to escape the nervous strain of negotiating with Metro, she accepted.

"I'm so tired and fed up with everything," she wrote. "I have had quarrels with Metro-Goldwyn, have had to have recourse to a manager and tried to discuss things with him, though I haven't an idea how they ought to be managed. I have become so nervous here, that one fine day I'll end by making a scandal and throw it all up."

Edington suggested a compromise that assured her of a salary twice what she had been getting before, provided that she agreed to start the new film.

The financial aspect was undoubtedly not the chief cause of the quarrel, but now that the company could be said to have come halfway to meet her, Garbo wanted to be equally accommodating, even though she disliked the part and had still not recovered from the exertions of making her first three films.

Vanity Fair's brilliant film reporter, the former hobo Jim Tully, was on the set while the first scenes were being shot and he has given a good picture of her: "The most famous Swedish girl since the days of Jenny Lind and Christine Nilsson."

> The Swedish film actress is phlegmatic, even apathetic. Of the fire that sets the white screen ablaze only the ash is visible in ordinary life. She is broad-shouldered, flat-chested, awkward in her movements. Her figure is the seamstress's despair. She has no real beauty, but with clever lighting and photographing, and good make-up that makes her lips more full and her eyes more narrow, she becomes graceful and fascinating on the screen. This affectedly sad, languid, indifferent girl is vibrant with inner life. She has a power to charm men and women. Thousands have been called the Sarah Bernhardt of the films, but Greta Garbo is one of the few who deserve to be mentioned in the same breath as that dynamic French Jewess.
>
> Garbo is the only woman in the world who has made capital out of her anemia. On the screen her indolent gait and half-shut eyes give an impression of exotic sensuality. The real

reason for them is tiredness. She is just no longer able to keep her mouth shut or her eyes open. She is continually interrupting filming with "I am tired, I must lie down a bit."

No one must watch while she is filming, and she loathes physical exertion. She won't walk a step—not even from her dressing room to the set, twenty yards.

At first they thought this tiredness was a pose—"I must lie down a bit" became a catchword—but medical examination has shown that unfortunately it is genuine. And so they are nicer now to Garbo in the studios. She is tended like a valuable animal.

Some weeks after Tully visited her, Garbo became really ill and had to go to the hospital to be cured of her anemia. A month later, when she was on her feet again, she wrote: "I have been ill, have worked dreadfully fast and hard. I can't sleep and as a result am fearfully nervous, feel tired and uninterested in everything; but, thank goodness, I am young and hope this will change. In *Love* I have a son of eleven. Amusing?"

In the studio, a surprise awaited her. They had run through the scenes that had been taken and come to the conclusion that they could not continue production as the film stood. Buchowetzky left in a huff and was replaced by Edmund Goulding, who redid the script. Lionel Barrymore was replaced by Brandon Hurst, and as thousands of indignant movie-goers had written threatening to boycott Metro's films if they weren't to see more of the couple Gilbert-Garbo, so Cortez' place was taken by John Gilbert.

After Garbo's illness everything was done to make the work easier for her. A movable dressing room on wheels was made, and in this she could rest on a comfortable sofa between takes. She was called a big star and given a stand-in, a French girl with the same measurements and sufficiently like her to be used in occasional remote takes. Garbo was relieved of the tiring lighting tests before takes and the fittings with tailor and dressmaker, which had always got on her nerves.

There is no doubt that Metro's wardrobe expert, André Ani, must have heaved a sigh of relief too. He found her troublesome and considered her taste in clothes extreme and provincial. If she wanted to wear a long dress in a scene, he thought she ought to be in a short one, and vice versa. Furs, which were supposed to photograph well, she loathed.

The film that was scrapped cost Metro $200,000 and production had to be speeded up so as not to make the new film too expensive. And now all went quickly. Goulding was not only a good organizer, but since he himself had acted in London, he knew the right way to handle actors. There were never any differences of opinion when he had to make scenes for Garbo and Gilbert. Neither wished to come before the other, neither had a special "side" that had to be given preference. With full-lengths it was best to have Garbo sitting or lying—that made Gilbert seem taller—and in close-ups he was "blocked," that is to say, put on a stool that gave him a few extra inches.

In *Love* Garbo no longer found work a burden especially with her electrifying and stimulating partner back.

John Gilbert, however, had not changed and, in private, as a lover, he could be very difficult indeed. At this time Garbo, who was again living in a hotel, received a visit from an old friend from Sweden. One morning, after a rough night, Gilbert rushed into her hotel brandishing a revolver and announcing that he intended to shoot her. Garbo was immediately warned.

"Just say that I'm not here," she told her Swedish guest. "I'll hide in the closet."

"On the contrary," said the Swede, "*I'll* hide and you say that I'm not here."

Gilbert had a tendency to identify himself with the part he was playing and this sometimes led him into doing very naïve things. While making *Love* he dismissed his entire staff and replaced them with Russian-born servants, who wore national dress and served caviar and vodka while a balalaika orchestra played.

Goulding's rewriting of the script had altered Garbo's part and made it more in line with her taste. With Karenin now a thorough scoundrel, instead of the dry, strict official of the novel, Garbo is forced to go and seek the protection of someone else, and Vronsky-Gilbert did not need to be asked twice. He finds her during a wolf hunt, blinks expressively in the direction of the camera, where Garbo is, and then attacks the savage beasts with his whip. He kisses his partner in many attitudes and many uniforms, dances mazurkas and, as usual, is frankly, uninhibitedly sensual.

Garbo got special recognition for the scene where she kisses Vronksy's sword, and for the end, where she throws herself in front of the train. The caption was: "It is finished —it had to be."

No vamp would ever have made such rational penance for her sins. Garbo had at last got out of playing the temptress.

Chapter 12

A SPLENDID LAND

No FILM STAR, with the possible exception of Valentino, had achieved such extensive popularity as Garbo after only four films. Shopgirls and secretaries stopped being skittish à la Clara Bow and became white-faced, tired of life and stamped with destiny. After this in shops, a customer's query might well be answered with a tragic shake of the head and a deep sigh—"it was finished." The businessman who told his secretary to type an urgent letter might be given a languishing look through half-closed lids that said more distinctly than any words, "I'm tired. I want to lie down a bit." The poor husband who found his wife's behavior peculiar and asked her if she wasn't happy, might receive the response of raised eyebrows and an enigmatic smile.

In France the type was called "garboesque" and when the press started giving advice on how to become a Garbo girl, Metro's own dress designer, Gilbert Adrian, provided the following recipe:

An absolute prerequisite is a tall slender figure without accentuated hips—those without don't bother. The Garbo girl should begin her day in pajamas of bright colors and over them a wrapper of black silk with heavy Chinese embroidery; that is, she should be rather exotic in the morning. The Garbo girl must shun lace and frills and negligées like the plague. Little fluttering pink ribbons and sweet bits of swan's down are quite simply criminal. Such things are for sweet girls and Garbo isn't a sweet girl.

In the forenoon the Garbo girl will go for a walk in a simple, chic tweed coat and skirt with a correct blouse or jumper—the whole with a hint of the "sportiness" that Michael Arlen speaks of in *The Green Hat*. Apropos hats, this too must be simple and sporty and the hair drawn back. In no circumstances is an unruly fuzz at the ears permitted. Large pearl earrings are recommended, however.

The Garbo girl spends her afternoon in a long-sleeved, discreet dress of crêpe-de-chine or flowered satin, but in the evening she lets her elegance blossom forth in full. Gala dress should be of velvet, soft silk, moiré or even lace; taffeta and tulle are strictly forbidden, as are puffs and flounces. Instead she will have drapes and scarves to wind round her neck. The dress should be cut generously deep, especially at the back. On top of all this elegance a cape of ermine or gold lamé, and thus equipped the Garbo girl will set out for fresh conquests! Chère madame, if you look garboish, dress accordingly.

To be à la Garbo became a craze. Her films were successful everywhere and Metro felt that they could base the next production on her alone. Gilbert was very expensive.

Garbo's new partner was to be Lars Hanson, who had done well in *The Flesh and the Devil*. Garbo's request that Sjöström should direct the film was granted and the very title of the film, *The Divine Woman*, shows that they had considered her wishes even on that point.

Sjöström found Garbo to be a perfect leading lady. "She

was simple and natural, quite without caprice; her conscientiousness quite exemplary. She never once came to the set without having prepared herself thoroughly down to the last detail, and if one gave her directions, she accepted them gladly, though she was a big star even then."

Journalists and autograph hunters besieged the studio from morning till night; there was more fuss about her than ever and people refused to leave her in peace. This got on her nerves and sometimes made her unwittingly hurt people. Once, when she was at the Sjöströms', the maid who was serving coffee happened to stare at her a bit inquisitively. "What are you staring at?" Garbo said irritably. "Go away." Mrs. Sjöström was appalled, because servants were as difficult to get then as now.

When the two Sjöström children knew that Aunt Greta was going to be at home, they would bring the entire class back with them. A peep through the keyhole cost ten cents and Garbo's cigarette butts fetched up to twenty-five cents when auctioned in the school yard.

The Divine Woman was originally a story dealing with the life of the divine Sarah Bernhardt. It was based on the great actress's career and the part made Garbo happy. The producer, Irving Thalberg, was not in Hollywood, and Erich Pommer was engaged to take his place. Pommer and Sjöström together worked out a script that Thalberg rejected outright when he returned. A fresh synopsis was made with the same result. "Boring," Thalberg barked. Pommer became irritated and resigned.

"It's no lie," Sjöström reported afterward, "when I say that I and Metro's own script writer, Frances Marion, wrote the story eight times before it was accepted. By that time nothing remained of the original material and every trace of the divine

Sarah had been obliterated. Instead, she had been debased to a pretty ordinary shopgirl who falls in love with a soldier —we made him that because uniforms suit Lars. For her sake the soldier steals a dress and lands himself in prison. While he is there, Garbo is tempted by a theatrical director with parts and a bank account, but it all ends happily after the poor girl has unsuccessfully attempted to commit suicide."

Sjöström was glad to have that splendid actor from New York, Lowell Sherman, play the theater director, and from the start Grabo displayed all her talent in the part.

"I had written a long monologue for her," Sjöström went on, "which she naturally spoke in Swedish as it was of course a silent film. There were lots of people on the set then and Garbo asked me to have a sheet hung up, so that no one could see her. Then she began to rehearse. On the other side of the sheet Lowell Sherman stood with the rest, listening intently. After the first take he came up to me and said, 'I don't understand a word of your language, but I can tell that that girl is uncannily gifted.'"

It was a very pleasant production. It was Garbo's and Hanson's third picture together; they knew each other's way of acting and fitted in without difficulty. She found Hanson as charming as when they had made *Gösta Berling* together and he was far from insensible to her attraction.

Hanson too longed for home, but making that film was almost like filming at home, with Garbo, Hanson and Sjöström all chattering away in Swedish.

"At the preview," Sjöström said, "the management came up and paid me a few compliments, but on our way home my wife sat quite silent. 'Why don't you say something?' I finally asked, rather irritated. 'Since you want to know, I'll tell you,' she replied. 'You shouldn't make films like that, Victor.' But it was a big financial success and an even greater success for Garbo."

Films now followed one after the other. Garbo's salary was enormous and they couldn't afford to let her be idle. To her great disappointment, Sjöström was unable to direct any of them. He had decided to return to Sweden, so that his daughters might grow up there.

Earlier, when Garbo once went to see Mrs. Sjöström, the two of them indulged in an orgy of homesickness, like a couple of girls at a boarding school. They pulled down the blinds to keep out the Californian sun, lit a fire and pretended that it was snowing outside and that they had just come back from a bracing ski run. Sjöström looked a bit surprised when he came home and found hot pork and peas for dinner.

Garbo mourned that now she had no one to speak Swedish with in the studio, for Lars Hanson also had gone home. He had been seized with an irresistible urge to tread the boards of a Swedish stage. In one of her letters she wrote, "I haven't met a single Swede for weeks. I have been alone practically every evening. I go nowhere, just sit and look. I must get home next year. Oh, what great deep breaths I'll take! I live the sort of life a seventy-year-old would like. . . ."

Her partner in her new film was an Englishman, Conrad Nagel. Fred Niblo directed it and did his usual excellent work with fights, railway-station scenes with trains arriving and departing, and that sort of thing. *The Mysterious Lady* was a thriller, the story of a woman spy who shoots the chief of the Russian police, steals various secret documents in circumstances of great difficulty and displays energy and efficiency difficult to associate with Garbo. One of the most interesting things about the film was the fact that the whole Russian colony in Hollywood took part—including a grand duke, a princess and a couple of generals.

Gustav von Seyffertitz, who played the Russian colonel, said of Garbo, "I had a big part in the film, yet very seldom did I get the opportunity of meeting and getting to know her. She was very shy and always sat by herself, somewhat disconcerted by her surroundings, or so it seemed to me. She was unassuming, yet possessed a mysterious power of attraction that perhaps was due partly to the fact that she was a foreigner."

There seemed to be so many sides to her that no two of her partners saw her alike.

Conrad Nagel didn't find her mysterious at all. "The best and most natural comrade I've ever had," he said of her. "She isn't one of those who thump you on the back and say 'Hello Mary—hello Dick,' that sort of naturalness is merely a sign of a deficient personality. Garbo had a very strong personality and she had the courage to show it."

Again the public raised its voice. People were disappointed at not seeing Garbo with Gilbert, and as the box-office returns from *The Mysterious Lady* were not so wonderful, it was decided to team up the two idols once more.

Had Garbo any suggestion to make?

Yes, *The Green Hat* had fascinated her as a play in New York. She would like to play that; she liked dying in her films. She particularly remembered the scene where Iris March drives her car against the tree with its memories of their love and dies, a typical representative of the post-First World War generation that liked to call itself the Lost Generation and whose great illusion was that it had none.

The Metro people were doubtful. Iris March was a British

girl. Could Garbo act one? The fact that so far she had only
been allowed to play Europeans showed how "alien" she was
still considered. But after consulting Michael Arlen, who not
only was enthusiastic about the idea, but even agreed to write
the film version, they forgot their misgivings. Leslie Howard's
role in the play was to be played by Douglas Fairbanks, Jr.,
and Gilbert was to be Neville.

John Gilbert's affair with Beatrice Lillie was still on. One
day she had an accident in her car and was taken to Gilbert's
house. She was not seriously hurt—one leg was numb and
she had a slight concussion. She lay on a sofa staring vacantly
at the ceiling when Gilbert, who had left the room for a moment, suddenly appeared dressed as Neville, fell on his knees
beside her and in a tearful voice, said, "You mustn't die, Iris
March, you mustn't die!" The temperamental Beatrice Lillie
recovered abruptly and dealt him a kick with her bad leg.

Garbo and Gilbert still associated, but only as friends.
"Here comes John simpering as usual," she said one day, as
she was standing in the studio with an acquaintance. It soon
spread to the public that the Garbo-Gilbert relationship was
no longer what it had been. People were accustomed to re-
gard them as lovers who did not need to act their passion
and they now refused to accept anything less.

Clarence Brown directed *A Woman of Affairs* (the movie
of *The Green Hat*), but it was no use. It was not another *The
Flesh and the Devil*. Garbo was excellent as the "shameful,
shameless lady" that Arlen had made of Iris March, half out
of cynicism and half in order to woo the public. Gilbert, however, was entirely miscast. A strict, reserved Englishman was
not a part he could act (there wasn't a less reserved person in
the whole Hollywood world) and he became dry and boring
as soon as he was not allowed to be himself.

William Randolph Hearst was famous not only as America's greatest newspaper magnate, but also for the exclusive week-end parties he gave at his enormous ranch. An invitation to one of those parties was the ambition of every film star and an honor paid only to those at the very top.

When Garbo received an invitation she decided not to accept. Gilbert tried to persuade her to go, but it was no use. She had no intention of going. He appealed to King Vidor and his wife, who had been invited too, and Mrs. Vidor, the actress Eleanor Boardman, promised to deal with Greta. She went straight to her dressing room and said, "Now what's wrong with you, Greta, don't you like other people?" A few minutes later she returned in triumph to announce, "She's coming!"

Each of Hearst's guests had a bungalow with its own staff at his or her disposal, and a program was prepared in advance that was followed religiously. All guests had to accompany the great W.R. on a riding trip, at the end of which they camped—tents and equipment being loaded on pack donkeys. Everyone had to watch the feeding of the animals in his menagerie: elephants, lions, tigers and crocodiles. A special attraction was a leopard that had a charming way of tearing bits of raw meat to pieces, and a python that swallowed small animals whole.

Up at the main building, that was more like a French château than a ranch, there were swimming pools and tennis courts, and more than forty sat down to dinner. Stars, financiers and politicians.

One wit said that the only absent one of all those present was Greta Garbo. It was about this period that she wrote, "Whether I'm filming or not, I'm tired and slightly unhappy and don't want anything. I'll soon be a little old woman. The others here are a bit piqued because I never go out and won't take part in their so-called social life. Perhaps I'll end up by living all by myself on a desert island."

As the Swedish colony dwindled, Garbo became more and more lonely. The Stocklossas, Sjöströms and Hanson had all left Hollywood; Svend Gade had tired of America and was working in Copenhagen. Then one day, a new Swede appeared in Hollywood. This was Nils Asther, who had been one of Stiller's favorites in Sweden and had acted in several of his films. Garbo felt a great need to talk to someone about Stiller and from Asther she heard how everyone had been amazed to find him white-haired when he got home. It seemed as though his intellectual powers had begun to fade too. He had shown no bitterness over having to return home without his star. "I hope Greta will manage all right," was all he had said. He had not done anything with films since he got home, but had put on a New York success called *Broadway* at the Oscar Theater.

They were looking for a new partner for Garbo, and she drew Metro's attention to Asther. He was good-looking, tall and imposing, and they agreed that he ought to make a suitable partner for her in her new film *Wild Orchids*. Sidney Franklin, who was expert at catching the exoticism of the tropics with its primitive natives and oppressive heat, was to be the director. The wild orchids were no hothouse plants.

Lewis Stone was Garbo's husband, a down-to-earth English businessman who slept well and had a sovereign contempt for all sentimental nonsense about love, yet, when he felt his marriage in danger, knew how to fight for it like a man. Garbo was hunted both by a tiger and a young rajah. The question was which seemed the more dangerous: the roaring tiger or the rajah with Asther's handsome features and rolling eyes. Garbo apparently thought that Asther was trying to be too temperamental. In one love scene, when he was pulling and tugging at her, she said, "Stop that, it's not a sailor you've got in your arms."

One day when she was in her dressing room in the Javanese bridal costume she was to wear in her next scene with the rajah, a messenger brought her a telegram. She read it and the blood drained from her face. She was found lying across her day bed, eyes half shut. They thought she had fainted and were about to call a doctor, when she got to her feet and said, "Tell them that I'll be made up and ready to go on in twenty minutes."

The telegram had brought the news of Stiller's death.

About this time Garbo had a visit from a leading journalist from Stockholm, who one day was invited to lunch with the great Mr. Mayer in person. The reason for the invitation was that Mayer wanted to talk about Garbo.

Garbo was Mayer's problem child. Apart from finding her too "highbrow" in her judgment of films, he liked her. But he was worried because he had noticed that she wasn't happy. Lately she had seemed thin and worn in her pictures. The company had done all in its power to meet her various wishes and yet she wasn't satisfied. He usually didn't find it difficult to understand artists, but where this Swedish girl was concerned his intuition and knowledge of people had failed him.

The journalist explained that Garbo had been depressed by personal sorrows. Her surroundings and the difficulties of adjusting herself had been a considerable strain on her, and, above all else, she was dreadfully homesick. If she could just go back to Sweden for a lengthy holiday, he was sure that she would gladly return and work for Metro again. Mayer

thanked the man for his advice and said that he would ponder the suggestion.

A week after this, Garbo wrote home to Sweden, "At the
present I'm working frantically on a new film. I'm not dreaming, making no plans. I just think how glorious it will be to
come home. It will feel like coming out from a lovely bath.
Just imagine being able to walk about in peace, round all my
old haunts. As soon as this film is finished, I leave the factory. Oh, how I long to get away from this factory life."

When she booked her ticket, she felt like a schoolgirl getting ready to go home for the Christmas holidays. Her joy
was not to be clouded even by the knowledge that a horde
of reporters and photographers had been ordered out to
watch South Pacific Station and all the places at which the
California express stopped.

She gave out a false time of departure and booked her
ticket in the name of "Alice Smith." With the help of a black
wig and dark glasses, she managed to preserve her incognito
as far as Chicago, where a film actor recognized her and
cashed in on his discovery by informing the newspapers.
Thus, when the train reached New York, the platform was
alive with reporters, all looking for a pair of dark glasses and
a black wig. But they could not find Alice Smith.

Alice Smith, in fact, had got out some stations before New
York and taken a car into the city. The newspapers combed
all the hotels, but Miss Smith had vanished. She had, in
fact, put up at the same hotel where she and Stiller had
stayed when they first came to New York. Thus, as the reporters only searched the luxury hotels for her, Garbo was
able to boast of being one of the few who have outwitted the
American press. The next morning she slipped aboard *Kungsholm* before anyone else and locked herself in her cabin.

A storm was raging and the *Kungsholm* had to wait four hours before the pilot dared take her out. It was no better on the voyage across. It was the ship's maiden crossing and forty-foot waves washed her brand-new decks, giving them a proper christening.

There were many prominent Swedes aboard including two of the royal princes, Gustav Adolf and Sigvard, who were returning from the wedding of Count Folke Bernadotte and Estelle Manville, daughter of an American millionaire. There was also an old acquaintance of Garbo, Captain Lars Ring, and he sent in his card asking if he might see her.

For three days she didn't emerge. On the fourth, when the storm had abated somewhat, she went for a walk on deck dressed in a black beret, high-necked jumper, a flowing ulster and broad, flat walking shoes.

"Good day, Miss Garbo," said Ring.

"Yes, we have met before, I know," Garbo said.

Ring was rather hurt. "I had the honor to teach you your first steps in front of the camera."

"Then I hope I've done you credit."

The mate came up to welcome her on behalf of the captain, and Prince Sigvard asked to be introduced. When that was done, he withdrew saying, "If you have any wishes, Miss Garbo, just let me know."

"Slightly better weather," she said, smiling.

Prince Sigvard told Garbo that he thought she should stop dining alone in her cabin. She asked where he ate.

"At the captain's table. You are welcome there."

The Prince had learned the new dances, the Charleston and the Black Bottom, while in America, and that evening when the band played he tried to teach them to Garbo. She was flattered by his attentions. Perhaps, in some corner of her heart, there still lingered the dream the little salesgirl from PUB had dreamt when she walked home by way of the palace yard with the hope of being seen by one of the princes.

On the ninth and last day of the voyage there was a snowstorm, which then turned to rain. The ship had been due in on the Sunday, but the weather had so delayed her that it was not till Monday afternoon that they caught sight of familiar land in the raw December twilight. But what did weather matter? This was Sweden and Garbo was up on deck and saw the first light buoy appear. She put her handkerchief to her mouth.

"May I yell?" she asked.

The press boarded the *Kungsholm* at the pilot station, swarming up a rope ladder. She received them in the ship's library.

"How does it feel to be home?"

"It's home!" She nodded, obviously moved.

"Well, your impressions of America?"

"But you all know how things have gone for me. It has been the same as anywhere else. One has had happy times and unhappy times."

Someone asked for an autograph on a waltz specially written in her honor. Absently she wrote her name.

"Write too that it's a divine waltz."

"No. I'm in Sweden now and I want to be honest. I don't know what the waltz is like."

"Tell me," another said, "what is it that makes you mysterious?"

This, they thought, she should not need to answer. Someone else did it for her.

"I think the most mysterious thing about Garbo is that she has bothered to become so famous, when by nature she is so indifferent to everything."

"What have you thought of your films?"

"One is always disappointed when one sees them cut and ready."

"Were you disappointed with *Love* too?"

"Yes. I should prefer to play quite different roles."

"Which?"

"Joan of Arc and Salome."

"And Cleopatra perhaps?"

"No, Pola Negri has appropriated her."

"What director have you liked best?"

"After Stiller, I suppose Clarence Brown. He isn't such a strong personality, but he usually gets a good result."

"And what American actor have you preferred acting with?"

"John Gilbert."

"What about Lars Hanson?"

"He's Swedish."

"And when do you think you'll marry?"

"I'm not going to marry."

Then the *Kungsholm* slid into Gothenburg harbor, the band played the national anthem and Garbo neither could, nor would, answer any more questions. She moved away and stood at the rail, biting at her handkerchief and waving. Now she understood what the Americans felt when they hurried ashore, that day when she first arrived in New York.

Chapter 13

HOME

GARBO ran down onto the quay and flung herself into the arms of Mimi Pollack, the friend from the dramatic school with whom she had corresponded while in America. They hugged each other, gazed at each other with tears in their eyes. Erik Zetterström and his wife, who had also come to meet her, urged her to get into the waiting taxi. People were beginning to call out and push forward. Then the enthusiastic crowd broke the police cordon and thronged around the car. *Crash!* Two of the car windows had been pushed in and the flying splinters cut Zetterström.

"Drive on," Garbo shouted, and the taxi moved off as fast as it could. Those on the running boards and cowl had to jump off in a hurry. The driver grumbled, wondering who was going to pay for his windows: "Send the bill to me!" Garbo's companion said gallantly and he got it—nine crowns for two car windows.

"I never knew there were so many people in Gothenburg," Garbo said, when she had recovered a bit.

The Stockholm train was due to leave in two hours, but the reception given her had been a shock and she felt too tired to travel further and so decided to spend the night in Gothenburg. She telegraphed to her mother and brother in Stockholm asking them to meet her in Södertälje (fifteen miles south of Stockholm) with a car, so as to avoid a repetition in Stockholm of the ordeal she had been through in Gothenburg. She didn't want to submit her mother to that.

They celebrated her return at the Grand Hotel and it was late before Greta and Mimi got to bed. The two took the Stockholm express the next morning. They sat in the restaurant car, chattering away over a glass of champagne. They both had so much to ask, but poor Mimi got no answers to her questions, for Greta insisted on knowing about everyone. How were they; what were they doing; had they changed?

"And you, Greta? Have you?"

"I? I can't change."

Photographers flashed their lights and the minutes passed as swiftly as the telegraph poles outside. Mimi had become the mother of a little boy while Greta was away. "What's his name and who's he like?" Greta wanted to know. A journalist interrupted them.

"Welcome home, Miss Smith."

Garbo smiled.

"Was it awful in Gothenburg?"

"No. They were very sweet really, only. . . ."

Södertälje in two minutes! Garbo was suddenly in a hurry, took her handbag and jumped out. A tall man and an elderly woman in a black coat came hurrying forward.

And so mother and daughter met on the dark shadowy platform, intermittently lit by the flashlights of the photographers.

"Where's the car?" Garbo wanted to know.

Mimi and her husband, who had also come to Södertälje, tried to persuade her not to go on by car.

"But why?" Garbo asked. "I'm tired. I can't face it. And then there's Mamma."

But when her mother also thought that it would be too cold in the car, she gave in and boarded the train again. They went back to the dining car. Greta was deeply moved and kept hugging her mother, while flashlights exploded about them.

Then they could see the lights of Stockholm and she enumerated all the new things she hadn't yet seen, the Concert House and that, and that, and that. She sat there, gazing out of the window. Then they were rolling across the railway bridge into the Central Station. "Is it really true?" she asked.

The platform swarmed with people all craning their necks.

"There she is!" "Welcome home, Greta!" "Three cheers for Greta Garbo!" People cheered, waved, tossed their hats in the air.

She stepped out onto the platform, thanked them all. Then, flanked by two stalwart policemen, she made her way down the platform and through the barrier. There the crowd's enthusiasm suddenly became alarming. A young girl with a frenzied look began behaving violently and so did a middle-aged man; but the police cordon held. As she got to the waiting taxi, she called: "Long live Sweden!" and the crowd cheered.

And so the car drove off with a tired girl, home after three and a half years in a foreign country.

Garbo told the Stockholm reporters that she had come home to do nothing but rest, twenty-four hours of the day, and she only wished that the days could be longer. But rest was not easy to get in the flat at Karlbergsvägen 52 which her friend Max Gumpel had got ready for her. Every magazine printed its version of her life history and her telephone never stopped ringing. The Royal Dramatic wanted her as guest star, UFA tried to persuade her to go to Germany, SF wanted a short news film, an actor-manager wanted her for his revue. She accepted SF's offer on condition that she could use the occasion to test her brother Sven, whom she thought of bringing to America. She acted as her own director and Julius Jaenzon was her cameraman; but apparently her agent thought it would be bad to have two Garbos in Hollywood, and so the idea of taking Sven to the United States was dropped.

It proved as difficult to find peace in Sweden as it had been in America. People wanted her for every conceivable kind of enterprise: a corset factory wanted her opinion of its wares, a perfumer had a skin cream he wanted her to recommend, a motorcar firm wanted to make her a present of one of its cars. Reporters watched and commented on every step she took—and she had come home in the hope of being herself and living simply and naturally.

One morning, at eight o'clock, there was a ring at the Lundells' door. (Mrs. Lundell was Mimi Pollack.) Lundell opened the door and there was Garbo in a raincoat. She had been out for a walk and now felt in need of a cup of coffee. She had with her a loaf of fresh bread she had just bought. "Well, you must look after yourself," said the sleepy Lundell, showing her where the coffee was kept. "And don't wake Mimi or the boy." The child was then a year old, and as both parents acted in the evenings, they needed to sleep in the morning. Garbo made her coffee and ate her bread and quietly let herself out.

She liked to walk in the rain, for then she was left in peace and could roam about her old haunts: Göta Street, Nybroplan, Djurgården. She was especially happy at being able to arrange things for her mother. She had often written trying to persuade her to move from Blekinge Street to a better flat, but she wouldn't. Now Garbo herself took a new flat for her on top of the hill with a wonderful view and still in her beloved Söder. It seemed that almost all the money Garbo had sent her mother for clothes had been put in the bank and never touched.

The publicity manager of the film distributors asked Garbo if she would let two eminent artists make sketches of her which would then be displayed in the foyer of the Palladium Cinema for the first night of *The Mysterious Woman*. She preferred not, but when she was assured that there would be no photographers or anything to worry her, she agreed. When she got to the place, it was half crammed with artists armed with sketchbooks and pens. As the publicity man led her to her place on the podium, she said, "You told me there would be two artists; but apparently you meant two hundred." After that she said no to all such suggestions.

It had become a tradition that on New Year's Eve the Strand Hotel gave a party for the elite of the Stockholm theatrical world. Garbo was glad to accept that invitation. Prince Sigvard was also invited and went there with his friend Wilhelm Sorensen straight from a dinner at the palace. The center of attraction was usually Sweden's most famous actor, Gösta Ekman, and he did not relish having to compete with Garbo. He was rather nasty and when he observed that she wore a white vest under her evening dress because she thought it cold, he remarked about it. Garbo told him that it would come off when dancing began, but she hadn't liked his comment. However, Ekman changed his tune and did his best to be pleasant, for they were old friends. The later it grew, the better friends they became, and he tried to persuade her to play a short season at his theater while she was on holiday. The idea interested her.

"But what part will I have?" she asked.

She was wearing a brown chiffon dress with a close-fitting hat. Ekman placed a candelabrum on either side of her and said with a flourish:

"Look! Lucrezia Borgia."

"No," said Garbo, "she was a bitch."

"Oh, bitches can be enchanting. I have several such in my portfolio at home. Come in some day and we'll have a squint at them."

The final suggestion was that she play Katinka in Tolstoi's *Resurrection*, and one day she appeared in Ekman's office to go further into the idea.

"What sort of person is this Katinka?" she wanted to know. "Not a slut, I hope, because I won't have that. Has she character?"

"Yes, in the first act. Then she takes to drink."

"And falls?"

"Yes, but rises again. And before that she goes to Siberia."

"That sounds cold."

"She has a man with her."

"I thought so. What sort of fellow is he?"

"I'm him. He has TB and dies."

"What was he doing in Siberia then! And she?"

"She rises again."

"In Siberia? Hollywood would shift that scene to the Riviera. More picturesque."

She promised to think it over and let him know that same evening, which she did, and even signed a contract. That done, she said she was hungry and, going into the kitchen, cut herself a couple of slices of bread and cheese. Then she sat in the pantry and sang Negro spirituals until the small hours.

Ekman came to her flat and rehearsed his part with her. Each time before they began, she said, "I don't know that I dare."

But after they had proceeded awhile, he would say, "Well, how does it seem now?"

"Yes, of course I can do it."

But he would scarcely get home before the telephone rang and she would tell him that she doubted her ability.

"If I'm going to have the courage for this, you'd better come and live here," she once told him.

One morning she called him up at seven o'clock and said he must come at once. She was in her pajamas when she opened the door for him and seemed to have lain awake all night.

"You know, I can't face it. You must let me off." It wasn't a world-famous star speaking, but a frightened little girl wanting to stay away from school because she had not done her homework. "You must let me off!"

"Well, I'll speak to the other two directors, if you'll go back to bed like a good girl." Which she did. "Sleep well, little Greta," said Ekman and quietly shut the door.

Garbo was a frequent theater-goer and now and again she dropped in on a rehearsal and watched her colleagues at work from some hidden corner.

Stiller's production of *Broadway* was still drawing full houses and one evening Ekman let her have his box, so that she could see it without being seen herself. This was the last thing Stiller had done. Its forced tempo and swift changes of scene well depicted the pulse of that great city and its philosophy that time was money and only money meant anything. In the restaurant scene an orchestra with expressionless faces hammered out that monotonous tune, "Ain't she sweet, yes I ask you very confidentially, ain't she sweet?" Behind the piece's lively orchestration, you could discern the grimace on Stiller's face; it was as if he had written his own death certificate.

After the performance, Garbo went to Ekman's dressing room to thank him for the box.

"Were you bored?" Ekman asked.

"No, no."

"You looked unhappy."

The next day she was seen out at the cemetery, gazing at Stiller's grave. She got in contact with all who had been in touch with Stiller at the end. She heard from his doctor how he had not had an easy death, and from a woman patient in the hospital how, two days before he died, he had sent her flowers and congratulations on her discharge, "from one who still hopes." One day she called up Stiller's old dresser, Runsten, and arranged to meet him at the corner of the street where Stiller had lived. Runsten saw her coming on the other side of the street. She halted, gazed at him, nodded gravely and walked on. "Presumably she regretted having arranged the meeting and found herself unable to speak with me," Runsten said.

There was an actress in Stockholm then, Märte Halldén, who had acted in several of Stiller's productions and of whom he had been very fond. There was thus nothing strange in the fact that she and Garbo had never liked each other very much. Garbo now looked her up and they soon found themselves friends.

Märte Halldén was one of those at the farewell party Garbo gave on her last night in Stockholm. In order to avoid reporters she had given out that she was leaving a few days later. When it was nearly time to leave, Garbo drove her mother home, then returned to the restaurant with a tear-stained face and a little bunch of flowers her mother had given her stuck under her jumper. She was overjoyed when Märte Halldén offered to go with her all the way to Gothenburg.

Chapter 14

GHOSTS THAT TALK

ON HER return to Hollywood she put up at the fashionable Beverly Hills Hotel.

Plenty of work awaited her. Her first film was to be *The Single Standard*. The male lead would have suited John Gilbert, but as he had married the Broadway star Ina Claire and thus destroyed the public's hopes of seeing him as Garbo's husband, Metro thought it would be unwise to team them up again in a film. The stir Gilbert's marriage had caused was reflected in the number of reporters who besieged M-G-M's press department when Garbo got back. They were determined to know what she thought of the marriage.

"Tell them," she said in reply to their questions, "that since Gilbert and I are good friends, I am delighted that he has been made happy."

The lead in the new film went to Nils Asther. He too had married while Garbo was away, but that did not matter in the same way. He had married one of the Duncan sisters and

Garbo used to tease him by asking if it wasn't difficult to be sure which of the twins was his wife.

Asther was eager to hear news of Sweden and especially of what Garbo had had to eat. "I'll kill myself with overeating when I get home," he said after a description of a smörgåsbord. Asther's appetite would have had a dreadful effect on his figure, if he had not been a bit of a sportsman too. He and Garbo often went riding together. He was impressed by Garbo's boldness; she rode so recklessly that she fell off once or twice and M-G-M seriously considered forbidding her to ride.

The Single Standard was based on an unusually sensible story. A modern girl who demanded that men treat her as an equal starts an affair with a fashionable painter (Nils Asther). He soon leaves her, saying, "If one doesn't want happiness to die, one must relinquish it voluntarily." In her despair, the girl marries a man she doesn't really care for, becomes a mother and, some years later, meets her former lover and is torn between her new-found passion and her duties. She is brought to her senses by her fair-haired little son. Mother love is shown as the one true thing—a woman's morality.

A young actor with a tiny part in the film was so paralyzed when he had to speak a line or two to Garbo that he stammered and the scene had to be redone several times. His name was Joel MacCrea.

After only a few weeks, life at the hotel became impossible. People would not leave Garbo in peace; and then something happened that quite dismayed her.

One day a girl in her early teens had come to the reception desk in the hotel asking to see Garbo. When this proved impossible, she began writing letters, telephoning and waiting for her at the hotel entrance. In the end, she managed to get hold of Garbo's manager. He asked her what she wanted of Garbo.

"I love her," the girl said.

Then one day when Garbo came driving back from the studio, the girl flung herself in front of her car and was only saved by Garbo's quick braking. The girl, daughter of a Milwaukee doctor, was sent back home by the police.

This episode gave Garbo a shock and she told her manager to find her a private house, as isolated as possible. Edington found a house near Beverly Hills. It had a swimming pool and was not on a main road, but it had one drawback: its garden was overlooked by the neighboring house. Through an agency Garbo found a Swedish couple to run the house. They had never had such a post before and were worried how they would manage all the parties and dinners someone with Garbo's position and money would be bound to give. However, they need not have worried. Working for Garbo afforded them more than one surprise. She never had people in and was always complaining about the amount of housekeeping money they spent. There was no cheating her over grocery bills!

The only person who came to see her was her manager, and sometimes, when work at the studio was over for the day, Nils Asther would come back with her and they would have coffee in the garden. Occasionally Asther stayed on and shared her very simple dinner, which was served anywhere and anyhow. On such occasions, Garbo would abruptly speak of Stiller.

"He was only forty-five," she would say, gazing at a chest of drawers that had been Stiller's and which she had bought among a number of other things at the auction of his belongings in Stockholm. On top of the chest stood Stiller's portrait in a silver frame. "He died at one o'clock in the morning. Only a nurse was with him. If he had recovered he would have started filming in Paris. He had pus in his lung. The doctors wanted him to go to Switzerland to rest."

Garbo seldom went out. Gilbert once got her to go to the Fairbanks' at "Pickfair," and there she met John Loder and his German-born wife. On her return from Sweden she had been introduced to the Belgian director, Jacques Feyder, who had just been commissioned to film a script by Hans Kraly. Feyder told Garbo the story and it was decided that this should be her next film: *The Kiss*.

It was, of course, Feyder's artistic personality that captivated her, for the story was a mere hotchpotch of her old films: *A Woman of Affairs*, *Love*, and a bit of *Wild Orchids*. Here too she was to play on the piquant, anemic theme and wear loathsomely luxurious evening dresses designed by Adrian.

The story was that of a twenty-five-year-old woman languishing in a marriage with a banker in late middle age. She hesitates to open her arms to the lawyer she loves, because the banker has a weak heart. Despondent and irresolute, she trails from chaise longue to chaise longue. She is adored by a young college boy and returns his love with a motherly kiss; but the kiss starts things going. A shot is fired and the bullet hits the banker in the back of the neck. Who fired it?

Conrad Nagel was to play the lawyer and Anders Randolph the banker, but who could play the young boy? A dozen were given film tests but none were any good. Finally, Feyder found a suitable boy in the Mont Martre restaurant —a young violinist called Lew Ayres, who was not only a newcomer to the screen but to acting.

Though he had a natural bent for acting, he found the first day's filming with Garbo very difficult. He was to come rushing in, look around and, the moment he saw Garbo, fling his arms around her. It was a difficult enough scene to give an experienced actor a complex, and young Ayres was panic-stricken and merely stared at the world-famous star. Garbo turned to Feyder and said, "Can't Mr. Ayres and I have a cigarette and a chat first? How can we play such a scene when we have never seen each other before?" Thus, by suggesting that she herself felt inhibited, she managed to calm Ayres, who hadn't words enough for Garbo's kindness.

"She is wholly unselfish in giving credit where it is due," he said. He emphasized, too, her total lack of egocentric temperament; whatever happened during filming, she remained calm.

Feyder was forced to introduce a number of cheap effects into *The Kiss*, which depressed the artist in him, especially as he admired Garbo and had long wanted to work with her.

At this time sensational things were happening in the film world. Warner Brothers had begun experimenting with sound film. The early attempts were more of a sensation than a success, but then came a version of *Don Juan* with sound effects and this was followed by *The Jazz Singer*—an unparalleled success—in which Al Jolson both spoke and sang. What people noticed most was that the dialogue came out better than the singing.

Other companies then followed suit: Fox, Paramount, United Artists. Metro hesitated longest, and when it was announced that they intended to make a "talkie" with Garbo, it caused considerable surprise in film circles. What a risk using Garbo with her foreign accent! Pola Negri and Lya de

Putti had already failed when they tried to venture into the field of "talkies."

The foreigners, of course, were not the only ones whom talkies banished from the film business. Many American and English show people shuddered at the new invention. For those with good voices it provided a wonderful new means of expression; it was now possible to do away with miming and the sweeping gesture, thus introducing a new style of film acting. But of course for those with bad voices the talkies meant disaster.

Many who, as long as they were mute, had been brightly shining stars surrounded with the nimbus of fame and the mystery of distance, were reduced to the lowest level of banality as soon as they began to speak. That was the case with Norma Talmadge and Colleen Moore; Douglas Fairbanks proved to have a slight, unmodulated voice, as is often the case with the physically overtrained, and John Gilbert's shrill way of talking was a real disillusion.

How would Garbo manage?

The company and she discussed a suitable part. What could be more natural than that she should suggest for her sound debut the part she had wished to play ever since her student days, Anna Christie, the sailor's Swedish girl whom O'Neill described as a well-developed Viking girl of twenty. Here her accent would not only be justified, but an advantage. When they started to film, her English proved to be so good that some scenes had to be retaken because her accent wasn't noticeable enough. Delighted at being able to act a part with which she felt in sympathy and where there was no need to be the erotic-exotic-anemic woman who wore an endless succession of evening dresses, she wore the same simple tweed skirt and thick-knit jumper throughout the film.

What was her voice like?

The first words she said, spoken as she entered Johnny the Priest's bar, were, "Give me a whisky, and don't be stingy!" They gave many people a shock. Did she really have such a deep, almost coarse voice? But people soon got accustomed to it and began to find it both personal and characteristic, rather like the sound of wind in a Nordic pine wood, or, in tender scenes, like the whisper of a soft summer breeze.

Very few shared the view of one English critic: "Her voice is ugly, throaty, raw and full of German gutturals." On the other hand those who had ears to hear and eyes to see, noticed that speech was a hindrance to her and tended to hamper her acting. But what character she gave to this girl whom a negligent father had forced into poverty and prostitution!

The scene with her father was unforgettable. Her face reflected the whole gamut of expression from apathy and half-suppressed contempt to icy disgust and hatred, changing to a child's despairing grief when her father has sobered enough to recognize her. Later, when Matt comes into her life and lets her believe again that it holds room for beauty, hope glimmers on that sorrowfully lovely face.

The opening scenes are suggestive. . . . Mist over New York Harbor and a dimly lit cabin in which the skipper's mistress gulps whisky in order to stop her hiccups and in between tries to sing down the sound of a screeching phonograph and the wailing of foghorns. This part was played by Marie Dressler, whose drunken voice and fruitless efforts to get her hat on her head are magnificiently done.

As Matt, Charles Bickford was a new leading man for Garbo. The red-haired Irishman amused her with his rough sense of humor, but when he wanted to introduce her to a friend who was an admirer of hers, she said no. She refused social contacts while working.

Bickford knew at first hand how determined Garbo could be, a thing the studio heads knew to their cost. If they tried to force their wishes on her, she simply stayed away from the studios until they agreed to what she wanted. Many stars have tried to imitate her, but none have succeeded. Garbo alone has been able to behave like that, simply because it was in keeping with her character.

The others in the film, like Bickford, were eminent stage actors. Neither he nor Marie Dressler has expressed an opinion on Garbo as an actress. Marie Dressler found her phlegmatic in private life. "I have never seen her display any great interest in anything, except once, when I suggested making a film about Queen Christina of Sweden. About that she became almost enthusiastic; but otherwise she appeared totally indifferent to her surroundings, simply bored to death."

George F. Marion, whom many thought stole the film as her father, had the humility to say that she was "so inspiring that she brought out the best in those acting with her." He lauded her to the skies as an actress. "She has genius where characterization is concerned; she falls in love with the intellectual aspect of the part and by reason of this sympathy literally slips into her characters. In my opinion this is what is meant by real art."

After experiencing Feyder's mild direction, Garbo lost her enthusiasm for Brown who directed *Anna Christie,* and when it was decided to make a German version as well, she made it a condition that Feyder should direct it. She herself considered the German version superior to the American, which delighted Feyder.

Garbo was charmed by the Belgian director, who was a highly cultured person, and they became better and better friends. One thing still stood between them, the memory of a dead man, Mauritz Stiller, of whom Garbo had a strange way of speaking in the present tense: "He says this . . . he does so and so." Feyder used to call him "the green shadow."

While *Anna Christie* was being made, Garbo was often visited by Feyder and his wife, and sometimes, too, by the John Loders. One evening, soon after her guests had gone, the doorbell rang. Feeling sure that one of them had left something behind, Garbo went to open the door herself, and there was the girl from Milwaukee, now grown up and very smartly dressed. She smiled and calmly walked in.

"What do you want?" Garbo asked.

"Talk with you a bit and look at you—I guess."

"Will you kindly go this moment?"

"Now don't be silly, Greta."

Garbo called her servants, who had a struggle to get the wildly protesting girl out of the house.

Chapter 15

THE WORKING DAY

GARBO usually got up at seven o'clock and began the day with a quarter of an hour in her swimming pool. Then she had breakfast in bed, took her time about dressing, and then emerged demanding her car in a hurry, so that she could arrive at the studio on time. (She could never learn to back her car out of the garage. This maneuver had to be performed for her by her servant, Norlin.) Then she got in and sped off to the studio, where she would be made up and ready to go on by half-past eight. She always took a cardboard box with her lunch, which consisted of sandwiches and salad, fruit and cream, just like any little shopgirl. This she ate in her dressing room, never in the big staff lunchroom the company provided. On the stroke of five she left the studio, even if they were in the middle of a scene. She considered that she had to have her time off if she was to manage her heavy program.

Anna Christie was an enormous box-office success. M-G-M asked Garbo for suggestions for her next talkie. This was again a play she had seen in Stockholm as a girl, Edward Sheldon's *Romance*, a play that was damned by the critics but loved by the public all over the world. It was dismissed as sentimental tripe, cheap magazine drivel, yet drew full houses. It was a story of two extremes: there was the actress, representing the epitome of frivolity, and the young clergyman, the strict guardian of morality. That is a combination that seldom fails in its effect. It begins with an old, white-haired clergyman sitting by a dying fire with a young relative who has got involved in a romantic love affair. "Perhaps," says the old man, "it will be a help to you to know what happened to me when I was young." Thus the story is told and the film ends beside the fire again. It was good film stuff and when Garbo saw the play while still at the dramatic school, it had made an indelible impression on her.

Garbo wanted to have the same costume as the Swedish actress she had seen play the part, so they sent to Stockholm for the original sketches of the costumes. The great question was, who was to play the romantic young clergyman, Tom Armstrong? Gary Cooper was suggested, but it was decided that he would look too modern in nineteenth-century costume. Douglas Fairbanks and Mary Pickford tried to persuade her of the excellence of "Doug Junior," but Garbo was always against nepotism, considering that people must get along by their own efforts and ability. They made film tests and thumbed the photographs in the agents' registers. One day, while doing so, Garbo exclaimed, "*He* could play Armstrong."

The "he" proved to be a young English actor whose road to fame is itself a film story. Gavin Gordon had staked all to go to Hollywood in order to act with his ideal, Greta Garbo. Then, on his way to one of the first takes, he had an automobile accident and broke his collarbone. A doctor was summoned, and he vainly tried to prevent Gordon from going on to the studio. Gordon insisted, however. After some hours' work, he dropped unconscious in front of the camera. Garbo was so impressed by his courage that, although production had scarcely begun, she got them to work on the other scenes until Gordon could continue.

Thus Gordon had every reason to like Garbo. He is one of those who respected her and considered that ordinary mortals deserved only to admire her from a distance. "If I had," he once said, "the dynamic personality of a David, the gifts of Sophocles and the appearance of Apollo, I should perhaps dare to endeavor to win Garbo's attention and favors!"

Garbo was very particular about the text of her parts and this often led to quite vehement differences of opinion between her and the director and producer. In this film, the heroine's servant was played by Marjorie Rambeau, who owned the Pekingese which was Garbo's dog in the film. Garbo wanted a change made in one scene. The producer, director and even the scenario writers were summoned. All insisted that the scene must be played as it was. Garbo turned to Marjorie Rambeau and said, "May I borrow your dog?"

"Why?"

"He has to pee."

"I don't think so."

"Yes, indeed."

"Well—"

Garbo took the dog and went out, followed some minutes later by one of the assistants.

"Will you please come in, Miss Garbo?"

"No. The dog has to pee."

Five minutes later the assistant director came out. "May I ask you to come in, Miss Garbo?"

"No, the dog hasn't peed yet."

Finally Clarence Brown himself came out. "Greta, please! You can have your way."

"All right. Now the dog has peed."

Garbo thought Gordon convincing and unaffected as Armstrong and felt that the film turned out badly because of her deplorable Italian accent. But the real reason was that she did not fit the nineteenth-century theme. Her broad shoulders and slow movements did not go with Rita Cavallini's crinoline, even though her voice sounded southern enough and spoke of past erotic delights and promised new.

This relative failure makes it all the more remarkable that Metro followed *Romance* with an almost identical story in *Inspiration.* As one critic said of it, it was so little inspired or inspiring that it ought to have had a different title. It was a banal, sentimental plagiarism of the stories of *Bohème* and *La Dame aux Camélias,* depicting a world of money-hungry cocottes, blasé and world-weary, who always had rich and jealous lovers.

Robert Montgomery, who was the one they favored most as the lover, thought it every actor's dream to act with Garbo and has said that he felt really "excited" when he received the offer. The actual filming was instructive and good training for him, he said, "for Garbo is not only a great actress, but also a woman with understanding and a sense of humor."

Lewis Stone, who was the polished, wealthy lover, was the actor who played with Garbo in six films. His opinion of her is succinct: "Garbo is an artist; as a woman she is never the same and so always interesting."

Garbo found Montgomery very formal. They had one scene

together in front of the fireplace in Yvonne-Garbo's drawing room. Before they began, they adjusted their make-up on the set. Montgomery apparently thought that the situation called for a jocular apology from him, so that he shouldn't appear too vain. "Don't you think, Miss Garbo, that this is a silly occupation for a man?"

"Yes, I do," said Garbo.

Then they were all ready. The camera began to whir. "I am very tired," sighed Garbo, while the artificial fire (from a bulb) shed its glow on them and the snowflakes outside the window looked as though they came from a dusty attic. "Very, very tired," she repeated. And she had reason to be so, both on and off stage, for she had now made five films, one after the other.

The company now granted her six weeks' leave so that she might rest. This was too short a time to go back to Sweden, as she would dearly have liked to do.

She received occasional visits from a sister of Stiller who lived in California. On one of these visits they went to a restaurant for dinner and, as was her way, Garbo chose a table in the farthest corner. There, she noticed that a man was staring impertinently at her and she deliberately turned her back on him while she chatted with Miss Stiller, a full-bosomed lady with a hint of mustache under a prominent nose. The man was not so easily put off. He came up and with a polite smile said, "You are Miss Garbo, aren't you?"

"No," Garbo said angrily, pulling her hat down.

The man turned to Miss Stiller and said, "Nor you?"

Apart from Miss Stiller, Garbo had few Swedish contacts left, now that Nils Asther had married and they no longer acted together. For a time she did have a companion in Mona Mårtenson, who was a fellow student at the dramatic school

and whom Metro had put under contract. But there seemed
to be no work for her and she was not even given a film test.
After six months, she packed up and went home bitterly disappointed. Garbo tried to persuade her to stay and promised
to help, but she would not. Garbo felt very lonely after she
had gone.

It was a pleasant surprise, therefore, when Wilhelm Sorensen, friend of Prince Sigvard, came to Hollywood to have a
look at the place just as Garbo was granted her leave. Garbo
had met him at the New Year festivities at Strand Hotel and
had christened him "The Winter Apple" because of his rosy
cheeks. She now asked if he would like to accompany her on a
holiday trip somewhere.

They drove together to San Francisco in Garbo's car. Wearing her dark glasses, Garbo registered at the hotel as Sorensen's sister, hoping she would be left in peace. Here her favorite occupation was to roam about the Chinese quarter looking at brocades and pajamas. She never bought anything till
she had paid at least two visits to a shop. Whether this was
due to her business sense or that of the Chinese, it is difficult
to say. She liked being in San Francisco, where she was not
recognized. However, she ran out of money and had to go to
the bank to cash a check. When the cashier saw her signature,
he stared at the girl in the beret, dark glasses and simple
hair-do as though in disbelief and he asked her if she could
prove her identity, which she did. At that, all work in the
bank stopped and young and old craned and peered; even
the managers opened the doors of their offices to see her.

"Ugh, it was most unpleasant," she told Sorensen when
she got back to the hotel. She went up to her room, leaving
Sorensen downstairs. When he finally stepped into the elevator, the elevator boy said, "Wasn't that Greta Garbo?"

"No," Sorensen said.

"But I'm quite sure it was."

"No, it was my sister."

"Don't try to fool me," said the boy in good Stockholm slang. "I saw her myself on Nybroplan last year."

Next, the telephone rang and the operator said there was a call for Miss Sorensen. "She's not in," Sorensen replied. "Could she perhaps let me know when she comes in?" the operator asked. Garbo took the receiver. The operator begged her pardon for troubling her; she had merely wanted to hear Miss Garbo's voice!

It was evidently time to leave San Francisco.

Garbo spent the rest of her holiday on a ranch out in the desert at La Quinta, where she rented a bungalow with three rooms and a kitchen, and there she sun-bathed and read.

The public taste in film heroes was changing. It had already swung away from the beautiful-featured type, such as Valentino, Barthelmess and Gilbert, to that of the perfect gentleman—Clive Brook, Lewis Stone; and now with the talkies had gone to the other extreme of tough young men with booming voices and bulging muscles.

It was now decided that Clark Gable was to partner Garbo in her next film, *Susan Lenox*. Gable was on the company's register as a "supertough guy," and having seen a film in which he gave a prima donna a smack on the behind, Garbo wondered how on earth she was going to accept that sort of thing. Some words in the script (honey, sweetie, sugar, etc.) were too much in the same style for her and she demanded that they be cut.

Alongside Garbo's studied femininity, Gable was almost comically uncomplicated, but the public found the combination interesting. They hadn't seen anything as masculine as Gable for a long time and the film was as great a success as *Anna Christie*. The *New York Times* stated: "Garbo no longer has any rivals; she is the sovereign queen of the films." The British papers were even more enthusiastic. The *Daily Mail*'s critic wrote that he knelt at the feet of the wonderful Swede and that, for him, they might get rid of all other stars as long as he could see Garbo. There was a real Garbo craze. The Prince of Wales, who never missed one of her films, went to see *Susan Lenox* three times.

The best thing in the film was its useful reminder of the tragedy of popularity. The German director, Ludwig Berger, had read the book before he went to see the picture. He met Garbo after the performance.

"Did you know," he said, "that last paragraph in the book might have been written about you?"

"No."

"Listen to this," he said, pulling a paperback edition out of his pocket: " 'The last time I saw her, she was just getting into her car, and I stopped to admire the grace of her movements. Then I saw her profile in the light of the street lamp. Do you recognize that profile? You see it in all who have succeeded. . . . Well, perhaps she was happy, but—I do not envy her.' "

Garbo nodded and said nothing.

Garbo still had a hankering to play Bernard Shaw's Joan of Arc, which she considered called for a European director. Feyder had had enough of Hollywood's concessions to the box office and returned to France, so Garbo asked Berger if he would be interested and if he thought she would suit the part of Joan of Arc.

"*Gewiss*," said Berger. "If you had been born in the fifteenth century, you would certainly have been burned."

But the M-G-M chiefs would not hear of witches or the stake in connection with Greta Garbo. Anyway, her next film had already been decided on. It was to be about Mata Hari, the dancer who used her physical charms to obtain military and political secrets during the First World War.

The Russian general, Shubin (Lionel Barrymore), is one of her victims. When he finds her in love with one of his own lieutenants, he spies on her. She is exposed, condemned to death and put before a firing squad.

Barrymore has confessed that Garbo exerted so strong an influence on him that every time he played a scene with her, he went about as though in a trance and that it was several days before he could get himself out of it.

Ramon Novarro had been chosen to play the lieutenant because of his fine voice—he was a good singer—and because he looked like a young Russian. On the first day he sent a large bouquet of pink roses to Garbo's room with a note. "I hope that the whole world will be as delighted to see the Mata Hari of the film, as I am to be able to act with her."

At first Novarro was astounded by Garbo's reluctance to rehearse. "She had a habit of just going straight into her scene —she always knew it by heart before she came. And the moment she began acting her whole being changed and the force she radiated electrified those acting with her. It wasn't enough for her to satisfy the director. Often—despite his OK—she asked for a scene to be retaken because she didn't think she had done her best."

Novarro and Garbo were an odd combination. He was one of Hollywood's smallest lovers and had a weak, feminine appearance. No heels, however high, were any help; no one could accept the illusion that he had bewitched Garbo or that anything but a strong maternal feeling could have caused her to die for him. Garbo herself was overqualified as the mistress and only barely acceptable as the spy. Her body was very obviously not that of a dancer, which was a great handicap in playing Mata Hari, yet she demonstrated how she was able to make herself convincing even in a part that didn't suit her. One of her lines spoken to Novarro could have been addressed to her audience: "Here are your eyes"—pointing to her own. Another line—"I am Mata Hari, I am my own master," had a very personal ring coming from her.

While the film was being made, La Argentina, the world-famous dancer, came to Hollywood to give a performance. Garbo wanted to see her, but hesitated, not knowing whether she dared go. A few days before the date, the theater called up to ask if she was going to use the tickets she had booked. She asked Sorensen, who was with her at the time, to say that she would not need them. Then, the evening before the performance, she changed her mind and one of the Metro chiefs was kind enough to let her have his box.

When the time came to get ready to go to the theater, it was discovered that Garbo did not possess an evening dress—she loathed long dresses and had never bothered to get herself one. Instead she put on one of her Chinese pajama tops and long black trousers and that is how, with face powdered white and hair stuck in under her beret, she arrived at the theater. She had not intended to attract attention, but as the audience consisted mainly of film and theater people, as many opera glasses were trained on her as directed at the stage. The first interval was such a trial that she seriously considered going home.

During the second half of the program she wasn't to be seen—she was sitting on the floor.

In 1932 the effects of the depression began to be felt in the film industry, and Metro decided to experiment with an all-star cast in the hope of enticing more people to the movies. Garbo, Joan Crawford, the Barrymore brothers, and Wallace Beery were all to be in the same picture. At once voices were raised prophesying disaster with all those stars struggling to get in front of the camera, stealing each other's scenes. But of course nothing of the kind happened and Vicki Baum's *Grand Hotel* became a milestone in the film industry; in it there was no star—all were stars. Vicki Baum herself wrote the script.

This was the first time that Garbo had played with John Barrymore, who was still regarded as America's greatest actor. She expected to find him a self-satisfied, puffed-up, attitudinizing actor, instead of which he was shy and not unlike herself. He talked shop mainly, and was humble and self-critical. Like his brother Lionel, he had a great sense of humor. Once, when Garbo ventured to say that another actor was good, Barrymore said, "There are no good actors. There are only bad ones who try to make themselves and others think they are good. Some bring it off, others don't; that's all the difference."

Garbo's part was the dominant one, but difficult. There was one scene with Barrymore about which she felt very uncertain. Before the take, Barrymore whispered to her, "I think you're the most enchanting woman in the world."

Throughout the scene she could feel him helping her by keeping himself in the background. Only a great artist could be capable of such generosity, and to everyone's surprise, at the end of the scene, Garbo put her arms around him and kissed him. Even Barrymore looked nonplused. Garbo and he got on so well together that Garbo departed from her usual custom and did not go to her dressing room after the take, but sat on chatting with Barrymore. He reminded her of Gösta Ekman.

One day Louis B. Mayer and Barrymore went into the sound room to study Garbo in action. She could not possibly see them, but felt something hindering her and was unable to concentrate. In the end she exclaimed impatiently: "I'm sorry, but I can't go on any more today," and left. The lost hours cost the company a pretty penny, and Mayer regretted his rashness; but as *Grand Hotel* was obviously going to be a hit, he did not mind.

Garbo and Barrymore were excellent foils for each other. Each day's take aroused the enthusiasm of the Metro chiefs for these two mature, experienced people. "She is a fine lady and a great actress," John said of her and, suddenly remembering his Hamlet, added, "and the rest is silence."

The première attracted great attention even for Hollywood. All the famous personalities were there to pose in the limelight and say a few words into the microphone. Marlene Dietrich was there, Richard Arlen, Patsy Ruth Miller. Polly Moran tried to be funny. "Hello, everybody," she said; "you too, Greta Garbo. I hope you're here, for my shoes are pinching so horribly. I wish I had your boats." For that remark she was hailed before the management and reprimanded, deservedly. Joan Crawford arrived with Douglas Fairbanks, Jr. But where was Garbo? They looked, they called her up at home. She was nowhere to be found.

The next day she said she had spent a most pleasant evening. She had put on some really old clothes, gone for a long walk along the coast, and had met a stray dog that trotted after her all the way home.

At that time Joan Crawford was at the height of her career; her part was a bigger one than Garbo's and she played it excellently, yet she did not arouse nearly as much interest as Garbo. One New York critic, an admirer of Garbo, ventured to say that on the stage the actress Leontovich had been a better Grusinskaya. This aroused a storm of protest from all the Garbo fans, but Garbo herself was the first to say that he was right. She felt that she had rather overplayed the part, but she regretted not having been allowed to stick to Vicki Baum's own character, that of an aging dancer who feels her star is fading along with her personal grace and beauty, yet clings convulsively to the enthusiasm she can still arouse in herself for her profession. Garbo was forced to make her fresh and girlish, but to ask Hollywood to give up its insistence on glamor was to ask the unreasonable.

Others rode the old hobby horse of her mysterious charm, but not Edmund Goulding. "I don't believe that Garbo's astounding success depends on any mystery. She has movie sex appeal, if I may say so, but her success depends more on her unique ability to work and her will to achieve absolute concentration before the camera. When Garbo says that she is tired and wants to go home—which incidentally happens very seldom—she really is exhausted. She feels that she can't give anything more and so would prefer to stop, rather than to do what she knows won't be good. The last time I saw her was in a silent film, but the switch to talkie has neither changed her way of working nor her personality. She was born to be an artist. Having once got in front of a camera, nothing could stop her climbing to the top—except unperceptive producers, of course—but they weren't as unperceptive as all that! For all her enormous success, she is just the same as when we worked together in *Love*; only perhaps a little more shy and solitary."

Shy and lovely—while the general public imagined her

sunning herself in her triumphs and conquests! "Fame hasn't made me the least bit happier," she once said.

Now, she had only one film left to make and then she wanted to go home to Stockholm. Märte Halldén had died. Letters from Sweden had informed her that she had become very religious toward the end, and that had made a great impression on Garbo. Her sister Alva was dead, Mauritz was dead, and now Märte. . . .

After the triumph of *Grand Hotel* Metro was keener than ever to sign Garbo up for another long period, but she refused. Her last contract had meant doing three or four major roles a year, which had been more of a nervous strain than was good for her and had caused her long spells of insomnia. Now she would only contract for one film at a time, if she could even bring herself to come back. But first she must get home and see Sweden while it was summery and green.

Metro continued the all-star idea of *Grand Hotel* with *As You Desire Me* in which Melvyn Douglas, Eric von Stroheim and Owen Moore also played. Never had Garbo been so beautifully photographed as in this picture, by her favorite photographer, Daniels. Her face shone with a translucent beauty. Daniels and his cameramen worshiped her. To make things easier for her, she used to go about in soft slippers which weren't seen in half-length and close-ups. Her constant question, "Are the feet in?" became a catchword; if they were in, then she had to change. One day as she was putting her shoes on, von Stroheim had a look at her feet. "You know," he said, "I don't think they're as ugly as people say." She loved that. Empty compliments and flattery she loathed; she was much too forthright.

The story of *As You Desire Me* was by the Nobel Prize

winner Pirandello. George Fitzmaurice made a rich film of it, redolent of that slightly decadent atmosphere prevailing in international circles after the First World War.

The wife of an Italian officer and landowner disappears during the war. Ten years later, his grief is as deep as ever. A friend—an artist who had once painted her—sets out to search for her. In Budapest he finds a cabaret singer who has lost her memory and who resembles her. She is neurotic and lives on stimulants in order to forget—what? The question is not answered. She is the mistress of a writer with a taste for hypnotism and sadism, who is using her as model for his new book. She wants to get away from him, and the artist has no difficulty in persuading her to come with him. She is just beginning to feel at home in her new (old?) surroundings, when something happens that makes her doubtful. "An atom of doubt is enough to kill a belief," she says. Is she Maria, the wife? Pirandello does not answer that question either. The externals do not matter; what is important is what happens in the characters' minds and here he lets no halftones or shift of emphasis pass unrecorded.

Maria was Garbo's best part to date and her best creation. Paradoxically, she had never appeared so sure of herself and free, but then here she was impersonating the work of a writer, not a maker of crossword puzzles.

Melvyn Douglas has said of her, "I have never played with a woman with such an ability to arouse the erotic impulse. The fact that an actress lets her partner take her in his arms or presses her lips against his does not make a love scene; you have also to see the emotion that drives her to do it, and it is this Garbo conjures forth at the right moment."

Garbo's part in *As You Desire Me* was perhaps that which

best reflected her own life. In one place she says, "There is nothing left in me, nothing of me; take me, take me and make me as you desire me."

The press bewailed the fact that this perhaps was Garbo's last film. A Los Angeles paper began with a quotation from Heine:

> Was vergangen kehrt
> nicht wieder;
> aber ging es leuchtend nieder
> leuchtet es lange noch *zurick* . . .

and went on to say:

"Why speak of a fine performance by Melvyn Douglas, or say that von Stroheim was excellent as always; why mention that it is a Pirandello story, when afterward all you remember is a woman going aboard a boat with swelling sails and sailing away into a moonlit night, leaving one with a sense of ineffable beauty."

Others wrote, "Garbo leaves Metro-Goldwyn with flying colors and band playing—and the public begging for more. Her acting is brilliant and surpasses all she has done hitherto —Garbo drunk, Garbo as a cabaret singer, Garbo a platinum blonde, Garbo sad, Garbo as young as a schoolgirl."

Chapter 16

STOCKHOLM—LONDON—PARIS—
NEW YORK

ONE night she stole aboard the train in San Bernardino; with her was Mercedes de Acosta the author, who had promised to ward off reporters and the public in New York.

When they got to Grand Central Station, Miss Acosta took Garbo by the arm and tried to look as though her companion were just anybody. Garbo was wearing dark glasses and a felt hat that almost hid her face. Together they strode through the assembled journalists toward a waiting taxi.

The reporters assumed that there would be a private car to fetch Garbo, and as a result the ruse nearly worked. At the last moment a reporter suddenly recognized her and the chase was on. Accustomed to following police cars chasing gangsters, the reporters had no difficulty keeping up with Garbo's taxi. They pursued her to her hotel and even up to her room. There she slammed her door and said bitterly, "Never again will I come back to this country!"

In order to spare her the attentions of fans—which meant brass bands, flowers and tears—a big notice had been put up on the *Gripsholm* pier: "Greta Garbo is not traveling in this boat." Just before the time of departure a taxi arrived and out of it dived a person in a gray coat and gray beret, pursued by a horde of reporters. Her mouth was a thin line and the world-famous profile pointed straight up.

She almost ran up the gangway where the ship's officer prevented the reporters from coming aboard, all, that is, except those who had orders from their papers to go with her and had bought tickets. That was an investment that did not give much of a return, for throughout the crossing she appeared in the dining room only twice, and then she ate with the captain and no one was allowed to disturb her.

Such a departure from America was severely criticized. One of the leading film papers wrote an article so harsh that it sounded like a recantation of all previous praise.

> President Hoover has the heaviest burden of work in the world, but he does not shrink from shaking hands with ordinary mortals; King George of England who rules an empire does not consider himself too good to appear in public; and that hero of the Atlantic, Charles Lindbergh, who loathes publicity, did not consider that he could deny his admirers' wish to pay him homage.
>
> Greta Garbo has left the country that has made her world-famous without saying good-by, without even suggesting that she was sorry to go. Who is she that she can permit herself such behavior? The world's greatest actress? Well, and what if she is? Sarah Bernhardt was and so was Eleonora Duse, but neither turned her back on the press and public.
>
> Isn't it time that America revised its ideas about Garbo? When the Swedish competitors came to Los Angeles for the Olympic games, reporters asked them if they would meet Garbo. "Garbo?" they said, evidently surprised. "We have

come here to meet the world's best athletes, not Garbo." Her own countrymen have never seen her in the supernatural light with which we in the United States have all too readily surrounded her.

Crowned heads, millionaires, famous writers visiting Hollywood have expressed desires to meet Garbo. She has refused. Who is she, we ask, to presume to behave like that? She refused to meet Lady Mountbatten when she visited the studios, refused to meet a royal personage from her own country, refused to have tea with Marlene Dietrich. And to nice, spontaneous Joan Crawford whose dressing room for many years was next to hers in Metro's star corridor, she has in all that time addressed scarcely a dozen words. When Joan Crawford was still Billie Cassin she danced in a night club, but before Garbo became an actress, she stood behind a counter in a store—is that so much better?

Well, now she has gone. Among her baggage is a fine leather handbag—a present from Metro's production chief Irving Thalberg—which contains the paltry two million dollars she has saved up in dreadful Hollywood. The new contract she was offered was for $15,000 a week, but she refused to sign it. Good-by—Garbo!

She reached Gothenburg early in August, 1932. With her was her brother Sven, who had come aboard. Through him the press had asked her for an interview. She shook her head.

"No, Sven. I want to be let off. I can't manage it."

"But wouldn't it be better to do it now—and get it over?"

"Are there many of them?"

"Not too bad."

She hesitated. Then she said:

"All right, ask them to wait in the saloon."

On Garbo's previous visit home, there had only been a dozen Swedish journalists to interview her, now there were five times as many, most of them foreigners. She was wearing a gray beret, pulled down in front, a lemon-yellow jumper, gray skirt and gray walking shoes. She walked very briskly. There was nothing left of the rather jaunty girl of four years ago. She looked hesitantly at the crowd of press men and shrank back as the photographers flashed their cameras.

She sank into a chair.

"This looks dreadful."

"Are you afraid of the press?"

"N-no—but I don't understand why so much has to be written about me."

"But you've written your memoirs and they're published all over the world."

"I have never written a line. That's all pure invention, words put in my mouth." She hesitated. "To be honest, I don't see how it can interest the public to know what an actress does outside the studio, or what her views on food are, or what she thinks about people marrying."

That last seemed to be aimed at somebody.

"Do you dislike Hollywood?"

"I can't say that I dislike Hollywood."

She was handed a cup of tea. She lit a cigarette and did her best to answer the flood of questions. An Englishman asked if it were true that she was going to act in England.

She shook her head.

"No I am not going to act in England. I am not going to buy Kreuger's house and I am not going to start a film company with Mr. Sjöström, as the Swedish papers have said."

"What are your plans?"

"I haven't any. You get holidays too, don't you?"

"What will you do at home?"

"Rest."

"Just rest?"

A woman reporter from New York put in, eager-voiced,

"If I understand aright, Miss Garbo, you intend to return to America afterward."

Garbo's face darkened as she saw the woman who had asked the question.

"It was you disturbed my sleep last night."

The woman had banged on her cabin door and insisted on being given an interview.

"Oh, no, Miss Garbo," she said, "it was only nine o'clock."

"You ruined my night at all events. I had just taken a sleeping pill to get to sleep."

All at once she looked so tired that none of them could question her any further. They had to believe her when she said that she had come home to rest her nerves in some remote place, "if there is rest for a restless soul." She smiled and went out, taking her brother's arm.

At Stockholm, the train platform was crowded with reporters and photographers. The Gothenburg train arrived in the evening—no Garbo. She wasn't on the morning train either. Then the telephone began to ring in the apartment of Garbo's old friend, Mimi Lundell.

"Can I speak to Greta Garbo?" "No." Can you tell me where she is?" "No." "Is Miss Garbo there?" "No, why should she be?" "But you are friends of hers." "Yes, but one's friends don't always stay with one."

Finally, a personal friend of the Lundells and an influential critic called.

"Dear Nisse [Mr. Lundell], won't you tell me where she is?"

Lundell lost patience. "She's at Gränna waiting for the pears to ripen!"

The following morning the Lundells found a piece of paper pinned to their door: "If you don't write Garbo's address on this paper, you will die." This missive was signed with a skull drawn in ink.

At breakfast the telephone rang. Mimi Lundell answered.

"Hello," said Garbo's deep voice.

"Hello," Mimi said. "It's three years since we spoke."

"Ask where she's been," Mimi's husband said.

"Where have you been these last two days, with every reporter in the world hunting you on the telephone?"

"In Gränna."

It was a while before they could explain why they had found her answer so funny.

Mimi asked if she would like to come and meet some friends of theirs that evening.

"No," Garbo said. "Not people."

"But they are sweet, dear people."

"No. I won't come—I know how it'll be. As soon as my back's turned, they'll start talking about me!"

Garbo saw that she would not be left in peace if she stayed in Stockholm, so she and her mother, brother and sister-in-law took a cottage on an island in the Skärgården and there she spent some weeks of a sunny August, going early to bed and rising early, sunning herself and bathing and playing with her three-year-old nephew. There she recovered and began going in to Stockholm at intervals to see old friends. Smiling and sunburned, she turned up one day at Gösta Ekman's summer cottage, where she met Noel Coward, who was on his first visit to Sweden. When they were seen together in the city, the gossip writers at once began hinting at marriage.

"Well, why not?" wrote one commentator. "Two such tired people would naturally sleep excellently together."

Garbo took to playing tennis for exercise. Her partner and

instructor, Max Gumpel, hired all the courts at the Tennis Stadium when they played, so as to keep spectators away. Garbo only wanted exercise and fun and could not put her mind to learning the game. One day when they had finished, they found press photographers gathered around the exit. Garbo retreated and was smuggled out by a back door that had been old King Gustaf's private entrance.

She went to stay with Count and Countess Wachtmeister, with whom she had made friends on her first voyage home. She and the Countess went together to see Karl Gerhard's revue. Garbo sat in the front row and at first escaped notice, but when during the interval she went in through the stage entrance to greet Gerhard, she was discovered and in no time at all a press photographer and reporters reached the theater. They rushed in, the photographer with his camera ready, shouting: "Heads up!" Garbo was so dismayed that she retreated behind a tapestry and refused to come out till the press men had gone.

"But Garbo dear," exclaimed Karl Gerhard, "were you really so frightened?" In reply, she took his hand and laid it on her heart, which was pounding like that of a frightened bird.

Each time she appeared in public, the press was after her and not always complimentary. One critic wrote:

> Having seen Garbo in the front row of the stalls at the Comedy Theater, I can no longer believe in her weary wish to be left in peace. Isn't there some neat hair-do that could tidy her hair a bit and make her look like a normal person? And is she so hard up that she has to keep her hat on and have her old overcoat on her knees? If so, she may be happy to know that I have deposited five crowns with the editor, so that she can observe our civilized conventions when she goes

out and not cheat anyone of the cloakroom charge. Neaten yourself up a bit and I assure you that no one will recognize you.

Yet those who met her in person were captivated.

One day she came to Wallengvist's studio to see his portrait of an actress.

"I felt from the beginning that Garbo had the modesty one usually finds in people of great sensibility."

"I am afraid I know so little about painting," she said. "But I'm interested."

"This was apparent in the independence of her ideas. 'When I think of Cézanne I see three apples on a plate,' she said. She pronounced Van Gogh with a strange *sch*-sound. I asked where she had heard it; she replied that she had got it from an American reference book with phonetic notation that she hadn't properly understood. But she became evasive as soon as the conversation threatened to touch on herself. I said that when I was in Rome and longing for home, I used to stand outside the cinemas where her films were on and look at the pictures. She wasn't flattered. 'That can't have been much help,' she said dryly. 'How lovely you were in *As You Desire Me*,' I added. 'An Italian film to quench a thirst for Sweden!' she said, shaking her head. Every time we met, I was more impressed by her lack of all pretense. She became the center of our circle, not because she knew most about art, but because she never used a cliché or jargon."

At times Garbo's mere presence was enough to enchant, as shown by this episode told by the writer Florén.

"I had never gotten to any of Garbo's films—one knows how sensitive illusions are—nor gone to any press reception, for I don't believe in interviews with her—she belongs to the element that is illuminated by the arc-light of eternity. . . .

A fortnight ago I went into the Grand Hotel. The elevator was engaged and while I stood waiting for it, the noisy vestibule suddenly became transformed into a cathedral, and when I turned, I saw Greta Garbo walking toward me.

"She walked like a princess in a royal cortege with head lifted high and an ineffable grace in her movements. I was aware of a feeling of immeasurable well-being.

"As she stood beside me, she was like a flame encased in a dark sheath—violet-colored cloth clung softly to her shoulders and hips; on her head she wore a flat blue hat like a Saturn ring—and her shoes were blue. I wished I had been those shoes. The elevator came. Then we were in it, a man such as I and the most beautiful woman in the world. Up we went, as though borne aloft on the mercury column of a thermometer; although neither of us spoke, we were aware of each other's presence. Her skin was smooth and radiantly white, her eyes were shining, her features classically pure; there was a contentment about her, a mysterious good-nature. I realized that all the beauty I had seen before, was but a pale reflection compared with hers.

"I stopped looking at her, because one cannot observe a phenomenon long without disturbing it by one's observation. All at once the elevator stopped. It struck me that she would never be my wife and that in all probability this was the last time we should ride in an elevator together. And then she had gone."

All the time she was in Sweden, M-G-M was negotiating with her through its Stockholm office. Metro had proposed that she do *The Painted Veil*, adopted from Somerset Maugham's book, but she didn't like the script.

In Hollywood, she had mentioned once to Salka Viertel that she would like to realize Marie Dressler's idea of doing

Queen Christina of Sweden, who also had been a strong personality, a woman who said what she thought in a deep, firm voice, dressed rather masculinely and stubbornly refused to marry. Viertel had now written a synopsis, which Garbo read and, after a number of corrections had been made, sent on to Metro as a suitable script for her. In the end, it was agreed that she should do both pictures, first *Queen Christina* and then *The Painted Veil*, the latter to be thoroughly recast. Thus, when she left Sweden in the late autumn of 1932 she had a new contract for two films.

First, she was going on a trip around Europe with Countess Wachtmeister. When their car stopped outside the Central Station in Stockholm they were relieved to see that not a reporter had got on Garbo's trail. The two kept to themselves on the boat and in London put up at the Washington Hotel in Curzon Street, where Garbo registered as Miss Swanson.

It was not long before the staff began to suspect who "Miss Swanson" was. When a maid one morning saw that her shoes were made in Hollywood, she notified the newspapers. To escape the ensuing hunt Garbo took refuge at a private address. One disappointed paper wrote, "Miss Garbo declines all publicity. Therefore we are not printing a picture of her. This is the smallest type we have."

One evening she went to the theater to see *The Merry Widow* and during the intermission went behind to see her old friend, Carl Brisson. The doorman recognized her and the next day it was all over London that she and Brisson were going to be married. The rumor spread like lightning across two continents. Garbo herself went to Paris, and never had a slouch hat looked slouchier than hers, or dark glasses darker.

But in Paris she found that she had merely jumped from

the frying pan into the fire. Wherever she appeared, crowds gathered—which is to put it mildly. On the Champs Elysées there was a throng like that at the storming of the Bastille. Countess Wachtmeister tried to shield her by staring back at people and saying in French, "Don't you think the people here look very peculiar?" They just laughed and went on staring. A journalist who tried to get into their car got his face slapped by the Countess, which amused Garbo and found an echo in the press reports.

> A public person who displayed such a definite aversion to the press and public would either be ill or quite simply stupid. Perhaps by behaving in this way, La Mysterieuse wanted to get herself still more publicity. An indication that that was so was her way of dressing. If she really had wanted to be left in peace, surely she would not have equipped herself with hats three feet wide, straw slippers and sunglasses, so that everyone could say from a mile off: "There comes Garbo!" Wouldn't a false beard and an umbrella have been a more effective disguise?

Others emphasized the diplomatic flexibility that Charlie Chaplin and the Fairbanks had exercised toward the press on their visits. They had given one big public reception and then been left in peace.

Le Midi made her the subject of a leading article. "Of course," it said, "there were obtrusive and unpleasant reporters, but hadn't La Garbo noticed that in France they were different? All the Parisians wanted was a smile, an anecdote, a gesture." But *la suédoise*—which in French also means a match—had not wanted to let herself be lit by their kindness, cordiality and charm. "Didn't *la mystérieuse* know that Louis XIV used to let people petition him when he was walking in the Bois de Boulogne, even if the only answer most of them got was a 'We'll have to see.' "

But Garbo was having none of it. She remained as inaccessible as ever—and the press keener than ever. One paper smuggled a woman journalist into her hotel disguised as a chambermaid in order to get glimpses of the star's private life. Yet each time the chambermaid came in, the private life had locked itself in a cupboard, instinctively sensing the danger. In this respect Garbo's nose is as good as any police dog's.

When she returned to America—in spite of everything—the Metro people emphasized the need for her to try to patch up her quarrel with the press. At the reception, one journalist joked: "So it wasn't only in America that the public's admiration for her art took such an uncouth expression as to include an interest in her as a private person." According to what he had heard, he said, people could be just as unmannerly in Europe. "How does it feel, Miss Garbo," he asked, "to be so notable that one causes crowds to collect everywhere?" She replied: "It makes me scared. I feel lonely and defenseless."

Chapter 17

A COLORFUL TISSUE

THE Christina film now was to be directed by that up-and-coming Rumanian genius Rouben Mamoulian. He and Garbo were agreed about how her part was to be played, but when she hinted that she intended to make herself up to look like Queen Christina, Mamoulian cried halt and had the complete support of Metro. How could Garbo want to appear with an enormous nose and eyebrows reaching to her forelock? Garbo said that Swedish critics would not accept a Christina who was not a real portrayal, and was told that they were not making a film for the history professors of a country with six million inhabitants. Metro wanted a film that could be shown all over the world; the film was bound to be criticized in Sweden, however hard they tried to stick to the historical truth, as Charles Laughton's *Henry VIII* had been in England.

The weight of argument forced Garbo to give way, and the Metro chiefs, who knew how stubborn she could be, heaved a sigh of relief. A worse ordeal awaited them, however, over choosing the male lead. They first suggested a well-known period actor from New York.

"No," said Garbo.

"Ricardo Cortez."

"No."

"Who then?"

"John Gilbert."

The film chiefs were taken aback; Gilbert was no longer in their good books. Voice coaches had been unable to improve his speech and enunciation—in emotional scenes his voice was inclined to become falsetto, which was enough to make a comeback all but impossible. Also, feeling that his career was over, Gilbert had taken to drinking more than was good for him, and was always quarreling with influential people in the film world and getting involved with the police. And how could Gilbert play a period role? Apart from his lack of technical skill, he was so nervous that he had to have a cigarette in his fingers to keep them still.

Then the Metro people thought they had found a way out. They would have a name that Garbo could have nothing against—the London public's favorite, Laurence Olivier. To get it all fixed, telegrams were exchanged and Olivier was asked to send his measurements, so that his costumes could be ready when he arrived.

When Olivier appeared on the set, made up and ready for the test take, he met a reserved Garbo in dark glasses. She remained unapproachable during the scene and Olivier, amazed, complained that she didn't respond at all. The scene was a most difficult one. He was to rouse her passion. If she thwarted every attempt to achieve contact, it would make him look very weak and colorless.

During a pause Olivier tried to talk to her. Finding her sitting on a trunk outside the sound hut, he began to speak about Sweden, thinking that would interest her, but Garbo only stared sulkily at the hut. He then switched to Queen Christina, whose life he had studied in order to familiarize himself with the milieu, and from that he went on to speak of acting. No reaction. He gave up.

Garbo looked up and said, "Life is a sad business."

The producers were forced to capitulate. Olivier was put into another film, which was rather painful for him as he had left England to fanfares proclaiming him Garbo's new partner. He departed from Hollywood feeling deeply hurt and for ten years he kept his vow never to return.

Garbo's new contract had given her still greater rights in choosing male leads, and she now assumed responsibility for Gilbert's making a success of the part. One day, before they had begun on Gilbert's scenes, he came to the studio to see Garbo. They had not seen each other for three years. When he stepped in, looking worn and haggard, his face furrowed and with shadows under his eyes, she was lying in her richly sculptured royal bed from the palace in Stockholm. He was now gray.

"Hello, Jack, I'm happy to see you," Garbo said. "Nice of you to look in, when you don't start till next week."

To the press, this meeting was more historical than the film and the reporters pounced on Gilbert as he left the studios.

"Well?"

"Leave me alone," Gilbert said. "I'm nervous."

"Was she the same as before?"

"She was exactly the same today as six years ago, and she always will be the same—just as bewildering. Three years ago, I could have sworn that she would never look at me again, and now she has fought to get me this part, when I am down and most need encouragement. Incredible!"

Gilbert's pleasure was genuine. He pulled himself together, read up on Queen Christina and worked and rehearsed hard. His wife, an eminent stage actress, helped him improve his speaking voice and tried to coach him, but Gilbert was not one who easily accepted instruction from a woman.

When he came to the first take, he was trembling with nervousness. It had not been possible to exclude the press—the management thought the publicity too valuable—and the reporters disconcerted him with their brutal questions even before he came on the set:

"How does it feel to accept help from a woman you have spurned?" "Would you have gone under if you hadn't been given this part?" "Are you thinking of getting a divorce now?" He had already tried several make-ups and posed for the press photographers, who tried to force him to produce his old charmer's smile.

When they began to rehearse he was already tired. It was the scene where the Queen, disguised as a young man, is compelled to share a room with Antonio. When it is time to retire and Antonio discovers with whom he is to share his bed, he exclaims, "Life is gloriously surprising!" The journalists smiled meaningly, but the producers were worried. It looked as though their fears were to be justified; Gilbert spoke his lines stiltedly and with a cramped expression. His nervousness affected his voice and the sound engineer reported that Mr. Gilbert sounded hoarse. Mamoulian ran his fingers despairingly through his mop of hair, but Garbo said calmly, "Let's have half an hour's pause. Come, Jack, I'd like a cup of coffee."

Gilbert kissed her hand and they went to her dressing room.

He was touched, but she told him not to mention gratitude. "Remember how nice you were to me when I was new here and felt scared and uncertain."

Her kindness had a soothing effect and aroused his self-confidence. After a cup of strong coffee and a cigarette, they began rehearsing again. Gradually his stiltedness left him, his eyes came to life and he began to act; but the sound engineer was still worried. In order not to make Gilbert nervous again, they put the blame on all sorts of things: a light had sparked or there had been microphone noises. It was only after several hours' work that they got a take that was acceptable.

Garbo said, "The part fits you like a glove, Jack!"

Mamoulian also spoke encouragingly, and after that all went well.

The world's most discussed pair of lovers soon found themselves back on the old confidential footing, though there was not the same playful tone in their association as six years before. Gilbert told stories about his little girl, imitated her way of speaking and walking, and made Garbo laugh.

One day he asked if she intended to stay in America now. She told him she didn't know. It wasn't the money that had made her come back, but a feeling of having no roots. In America she felt herself a Swede, in Sweden an American. Wherever she was, she longed to be somewhere else.

"You missed the Californian climate," Gilbert suggested, "for it can't have been Hollywood's social life!"

"Why no," said Garbo. "I have my friends here too."

Metro did not venture to show the Christina film in Sweden until it had proved triumphant in all other countries. The Swedes found Gilbert convincing, but not Lewis Stone. Garbo, however, seemed to have drawn upon latent powers.

She was especially moving in the farewell scene and at Antonio's bier. In the love scenes she was enchanting with her fresh laughter and waggish humor. One line in the film had given her particular pleasure. When the assembled councilors are trying to persuade the young queen to marry in order to save the succession, she replies, "No, I shall die a spinster."

When she had finished the Christina film, Garbo did something that set tongues in the film world wagging. Those who expected that because she had acted with John Gilbert again there would be a further installment of their old story were thoroughly disappointed. Instead she went for a motor tour of the Arizona desert with Rouben Mamoulian. The gossip writers were astonishingly free from malice, for they were convinced that this time the adventure would lead her to the altar. But the two came back looking as though nothing had happened. Mamoulian plunged into work on another film and Garbo was lost from sight behind *The Painted Veil.*

Garbo had now left her old house. The address had become too widely known and the peeping Toms more and more bold. There was always some man armed with field glasses watching for her from a nearby vantage point. A friend had told her that even her morning swims were watched. There was a skylight that she had never noticed and those who paid a dollar entrance fee to the servants could watch her from there.

Her new house had no swimming pool, but a tall cypress hedge made it impossible to see in. It was well off the beaten track. She was severely criticized even in film circles for the way she kept to herself. Nowhere was "personality" so much talked about as in Hollywood—books were written on how to become one—and nowhere was so much done to stamp it out. Afraid of being thought provocative and suspect, everyone lived and behaved alike, went to the same parties, patron-

ized the same restaurants, where they were all equally jolly
and hysterically exhilarated by a few drops of alcohol smuggled into their glasses under the table. Her new partner was
Herbert Marshall and he, being himself of a retiring disposi-
tion, sympathized deeply with her, especially as she was not
in the least reserved with him, but friendly and unassuming.

One day when they were making *The Painted Veil*, it began to rain and the crowd of extras had to stand about waiting for the weather to clear. Among them was an old actress
who was compelled to work as an extra to support herself.
Garbo happened to see her, asked that a chair be brought for
her, and led her to it herself. This caused a sensation, for in
Hollywood differences in rank are strictly observed. On the
top are the stars, whose addresses are Beverly Hills and
Palm Springs, where they live in houses furnished in "taste-
ful" style by a firm acting on the orders of the star's company.
Stars associate only with stars. They can always get a table in
a crowded restaurant. The next stratum below is that of the
stars' leading men and leading women. Then come the leading character actors, then the episode actors who are engaged
by the day. Many of them are excellent actors, but their
earnings are so sporadic that they must have some other
occupation, and many of them are waiters, night watchmen,
hairdressers or dressmakers. At the bottom are the extras, who
are never allowed to utter a sound during filming.

And pity the poor star, especially in those days, whose new
contract isn't quite as good as the previous one. Such things
are known all over Hollywood in no time at all and easily lead
to him, or her, not being invited to the right parties or, most
bitter of all, to being met with an apologetic "Every table
booked" in a crowded restaurant. Garbo thoroughly appreciated Beatrice Lillie's reply to a journalist who had asked her

what she thought of film society. "Film society? There isn't any."

The title of her new film, *The Painted Veil,* referred to people's tendency to see life through the veil of their illusions. For Katrin-Garbo life has to be full of the miracle of love. She is married to a bacteriologist who is sent to China where he devotes his time and energy to fighting cholera. His neglected wife thinks she is experiencing the great miracle with an official in the American legation, but he proves to be more charming than reliable. Marriage is out of the question where they are concerned, he explains, because if he were to become corespondent in her divorce, it would ruin his career. So she patches her marriage up. Herbert Marshall was the bacteriologist and George Brent the lover.

The scenario writer had not been able to catch much of Maughan's witty description of people and elegant storytelling. He had produced long, monotonous digressions that not even Boleslawsky's direction had been able to obviate, but at least Boleslawsky had managed to create a strongly Oriental atmosphere. From the point of view of production, the film originated a new style, and when Boleslawsky died a year or two later, Hollywood lost a promising talent.

Garbo had agreed that, while she was still in Hollywood, she would make a talkie version of *Anna Karenina.* This time she proved more flexible and effective than when she created the part. The famous mazurka, which she now danced with Frederic March, showed that she was more graceful than ever. Karenin was played by Basil Rathbone.

Then Garbo received an offer of $10,000 a night from the Theater Guild to act in a new play by O'Neill, but she preferred to go home to Sweden with a new contract in her pocket.

This time she found refuge in a cottage on the coast of Södermanland, north of Stockholm, and there she was safe. Her way of living had become more Spartan than ever. She got up at four in the morning—to the amazement of the local farmers—and with a basket on her arm went out into the woods to pick wild strawberries and bilberries. A farmer there still tells how, one morning, she saw his old father coming toward a gate and hurried to open it for him.

Everyone in Ånga seems to have found her simple and friendly. The little village shop had scarcely opened, which it did at eight, before Garbo arrived to buy bananas and apples and the "coarsest bread you have." That was her diet: fruit, bread and fish.

Ånga is a lovely little bit of Sweden. There are woods, cliffs and rocks, and sand to lie on, which she did all afternoon when the weather allowed. A hundred yards from the little jetty not a soul is to be seen, nothing but the sea.

Garbo felt she needed to rest and went to Stockholm only when necessary. She also went to see Selma Lagerlöf, the famous Swedish author, whom she advised against having her books filmed in America, as Hollywood would never be able to catch the atmosphere of Sweden or the character of its people. Mrs. Lagerlöf found her somehow "not of this world" and tiring to be with. Otherwise, Garbo visited no one, yet tongues were busy with gossip. She was going to build herself a house, as she was going to marry her Mamoulian, Max Gumpel, Gilbert, Wilhelm Sorensen, Noel Coward, Carl Brisson, and even one of the Swedish royal princes.

In the autumn of 1936 she returned to Hollywood.

Chapter 18

PRELUDE WITH COUNTERPOINT

AFTER Victor Hugo's Marion Delorme, Camille is perhaps the best known of the virtuous demimondaines of nineteenth-century literature. To the modern person with knowledge of psychology she is scarcely a credible character, but she has always been a favorite part for great actresses and both Sarah Bernhardt and Eleonora Duse played her. Already one film had been made with Alla Nazimova in the part and people thought that Garbo had a difficult task ahead of her when she decided that her next role should be Marguerite in *Camille*. But all the critics lavished unreserved praise on her and she was hailed as the greatest Camille yet.

Her Marguerite suited her age. Sarah Bernhardt's had suited the turn of the century, but those who saw her silent film found ridiculous her convulsive, eruptive courtesan with her violent sensual intoxication, interrupted only by paroxysms of coughing. Duse, quiet and subdued, emphasized the depth of the girl's anguish and her admirers still remember the tone of her voice when she spoke the famous line about the fallen woman being unable to raise herself, whatever else she might be able to do.

Duse's Marguerite was the poor victim of man's wantonness, a girl "led astray." Garbo's was anything but a martyr. She was the unsentimental prostitute of the day dressed up in nineteenth-century costume and with her hair done in corkscrew curls. She liked her profession, which both gave her physical pleasure and was a convenient way of earning her livelihood.

Never had Garbo been so gay as in this classical part of the great tragediennes. The scene where she dances the polka is meant to set off the first fit of coughing, but she made herself so gloriously fresh that one is scarcely aware of her coughing. Her laugh is so infectious that Dumas certainly would not have seen any resemblance to his model, Marie Duplessis, the girl ravaged by the effects of her profession.

When Marguerite-Garbo meets Armand a look of wonder passes over her face. What is this stirring within her? It feels so queer that she has to laugh. When he shows her the picture of his parents and says, "They have loved each other for thirty years," she replies, "Can one love so long—is there such happiness?"

She fights against the feeling; she doesn't want this serious young man to be drawn into her frivolous circle, but his kindness and tenderness defeat her in the end. She has to love him! Especially good is the scene where she has arranged to see Armand, but is compelled to receive the rich Baron de Varville instead. When the time for Armand's arrival approaches, she induces the Baron to play Chopin on her piano. Armand's insistent ringing threatens to make itself heard above the music, so she begins to laugh—a laugh so infectious that it allays the Baron's suspicions.

The climax of course is the death scene, around which Dumas originally built the whole drama, and here the skill of Cukor's direction is evident. While her creditors walk about valuing the pictures and *objets d'art* in the adjacent drawing room, Marguerite lies in bed with only one thought in her head—she is going to die before she can see her lover. Then her maid comes in and tells her that Armand has come. She tries to get up to make herself beautiful for him, but sinks back into bed. Armand tries to hide his emotion by kissing her hand. On the point of death, her eyes are alight with the wish to go on living and the smile she gives him is brilliant, till death wipes it out and she vanishes from Armand's tear-veiled gaze in a glow of light.

Armand, the pathetically naïve, is not an interesting role and though the script writers had done their best, Robert Taylor was rather uninteresting. One might have said of him, as one critic said of a stage actor who once played the part, "He made a suitable Armand, but he would also have made a Marguerite."

The only criticism of Garbo's interpretation is that she did not make people believe in the feeling of emptiness she was supposed to experience when Armand was not there. A journalist who was present while the film was being made reported that Garbo was always afraid of losing the feel of the part and the atmosphere. As soon as she was free for a bit, she withdrew to her dressing room, for her acting stood or fell with her ability to concentrate.

It is interesting here to compare her with another actress who played sexy roles, Bette Davis. She could laugh and joke right up to the moment the director said "take," then all at once her face became full of passion and she spoke her lines swiftly and impulsively. She had a complete technical skill such as only years of training can give. Garbo had to throw the whole of herself into her part, drawing on all her intellectual and emotional resources to achieve her effects. When she appeared on the set, she had worked out the scene in imagination down to the slightest detail.

Cukor and all her other directors have said how perfect she usually was. As she rehearsed, so she played, and she preferred to go over a scene as few times as possible in order not to lose any of its freshness, whereas Bette Davis could do a scene over and over again. There was nothing intellectual about Garbo's acting; she had understanding and great artistic intuition. When she was collecting herself, nothing must be allowed to disturb her, and the presence of even one person without business there always provoked vehement protests from her. When Malcolm Macdonald was in Hollywood and told Clive Brook that he would like to see Garbo in the studios, the latter, who did not know her, asked John Loder. Loder said, "Impossible! I know that she would never agree."

She had the corridor from her dressing room to the set screened off, not only to avoid being seen, but also to avoid seeing. In the same way, she wanted all the technical apparatus—camera, lights, sound mechanisms—screened so that she only saw those with whom she was acting.

Melvyn Douglas, a great admirer of hers, was well aware of her technical deficiencies. "She is strongly conscious of them," he said, "and is easily distracted by those who know more about the profession than she. As she is also very sensitive, she gets the shudders if someone watches her while at work."

Once, when they were making *Anna Karenina,* Frederic
March watched while they took a close-up of her. Afterward,
he complimented her.

"Do you mean, you watched me acting?" she said, horrified.

"Yes, of course—it was—"

"You shouldn't have done that," she said and went straight
to her dressing room.

It was because of this oversensitiveness that she never appeared on the stage. She did not dare encounter the public
face to face, because she knew that if inspiration failed her,
she had no technique to fall back on.

As an actress of world fame with a vast income, she stuck
to her simple, almost ascetic way of life. With her meals she
drank milk or beer, and only on special, festive occasions was
champagne produced. Her meals were served on her one service of blue porcelain that she bought from the Jannings before they left America.

She paid little attention to the furnishings of her house.
Her dress designer, Adrian, came there once and gave her a
few tips, and that had to do. She had two cats who could do
just as they pleased, but the toms that courted them were
pursued with the utmost ruthlessness if they tried to serenade
at night.

She still went riding and loved to go for long walks, especially in the rain. If the rain stopped too soon for her, she would
go home and get under the shower, which she said calmed her
nerves. She smoked a package of nicotine-free cigarettes a day
and thought that they had the same good effect.

She seldom wore anything but a tweed coat and skirt with
cotton or wool stockings. She disliked silk. When it was hot,
she went bare-legged or with ankle socks and sandals. When
it was cold she wore low-heeled shoes like a man's and of that

mahogany color which she jokingly said was "so practical for a bachelor."

She disliked scent and creams, washed her hair herself and seldom bothered to have her hair done. She felt best when her hair was like one big cowlick.

She remained very thrifty. Edington once told her chauffeur to have safety glass fitted to her car, and when her chauffeur spoke to Garbo about it, she said, "The old glass is good enough." "But Mr. Edington said—" "Are you his employee or mine?" So her old Lincoln did not get new glass. Whenever people saw the ancient car they said, "That must be Garbo."

Now, when she went to the studio after her morning swim in the sea, it was to play Maria Walewska in *Conquest*.

It has often been said that in this film Garbo was outdistanced by Charles Boyer, which is certainly true to the extent that dramatically and quantitatively her part was inferior to his, and it was so monotonous that she was not really interested in it. But Boyer and Garbo made an excellent pair and the intimate scenes between them were marked with a sort of sorrowful nobility.

Brown's direction was authentic, but overweighted with historical detail. The frame was made almost more important than the action. But there was drama and plenty of pomp and circumstance.

Garbo was always most self-critical. Whenever she went with the director and photographer to view the previous day's take, she spoke of herself in the third person. "Now she looks as though she were thinking of something else." "What a ghastly dress she's got on!" And when she went to see the finished film, she preferred to go alone. She was not in the least amused by other people's uncritical admiration or efforts to ingratiate themselves. Once she allowed Wilhelm Sorensen to go with her, but he was told, "You mustn't say anything." And afterward, her only remark was, "Well, that isn't worth much."

At the same time as they were making *Camille*, *A Hundred Men and a Girl* was being filmed, with Deanna Durbin. Garbo wanted to meet her young colleague and went to a party to do so. Another of the guests present was Deanna Durbin's partner in the film, the eruptive maestro with the face of a bird of prey, Leopold Stokowski, who, after twenty years of conducting the Philadelphia Symphony orchestra, had been enticed to Hollywood. Garbo went to see and hear the nightingale, Deanna Durbin, and met the eagle Stokowski, who swooped at her with all his virility and artistic aplomb, spiced with the smartness and speed of the Yankee. Garbo seemed bewildered; he was a married man, white-haired, twenty-three years her senior.

The reporters began asking leading questions and Garbo told them to "stop that nonsense." But when the two were seen more and more frequently in each other's company and dancing at restaurants, they began to be called "Garbo and Stoky." Then, when Mrs. Stokowski filed a petition for divorce, it was all quite clear: Garbo was to be Mrs. Stokowski No. 3. Their association became the subject of such vulgar curiosity that, as soon as *Conquest* was finished, they fled abroad and never stopped till they reached Africa—only to discover a horde of reporters lying in wait for them. Stokowski was not only famous in musical circles, but now every filmgoer knew him, and the two together were a grand slam for the autograph hunters who tore at their clothing, while press photographers disguised as waiters and chambermaids tried to immortalize their private life.

One dark night Garbo and her companion crept aboard an airplane bound for Naples, not far from which lies Ravello and in it the Villa Cimbrone, which, according to the brochure, was the ideal place for those wanting peace. It was almost true. Garbo and Stokowski sun-bathed, swam in the Mediterranean just outside their windows, strolled in the gardens where they could pick grapes, olives, oranges, and for a few short days lived like Adam and Eve. They went for jaunts in the surrounding countryside, and in the evening Stokowski played Chopin and Tchaikovsky on the piano in the hall.

The staff of Villa Cimbrone were accustomed to strange tourists, but Garbo was the queerest they had yet encountered. Wherever she was, she wore dark glasses, even while having tea in the shade of the loggia; she also wore the same pair of long trousers with a simple shirt or yellow jumper and a straw hat bought in the village. On their fifth day there Stokowski had to go to the nearby hotel to make a telephone call (there was no telephone in Villa Cimbrone). When he came out of the booth two journalists rushed up and asked for an interview.

"Why not?" Stokowski replied. "Ask me what you like about art or music."

The reporters wanted to get straight to the point, however. "Mr. Stokowski," they said, "can we come home with you and take a photograph of you and Garbo?"

"Garbo—do you mean the film actress? I didn't know that she was in Italy too."

After that a police guard was put on the gate and those who tried to get inside the grounds were hounded out by well-trained Alsatian police dogs. But the reporters had to send some news back, true or invented. The only way of putting an

end to their lurid speculations was to give them an interview. An invitation was sent and they approached the villa
somewhat hesitantly. The police and the dogs had been withdrawn.

They were received by Garbo—alone. She was pale, but
did her best to sound friendly.

"What do you want of me?"

"Miss Garbo, are you married to Stokowski?"

"If I were, you would certainly know it as well as I."

"How about a wedding?"

She shook her head.

"I have a few friends; Mr. Stokowski is one of them."

"If you aren't planning to marry, how is it you are traveling
for months on end together?"

"I am on holiday now—I have always wanted to see the
world—my friend has promised to show me some of the beautiful things there are." She accentuated every syllable, like a
nervous actress on the first night.

"We hope you have a pleasant holiday."

"One cannot have a holiday if one is not left in peace."
There was a pause. Then she went on quietly, "I am as I am.
You must understand that!"

She forced herself to shake hands with several of them,
thereby giving them to understand that the interview was at
an end. In reality she had said next to nothing, but it was
enough to jam the telephone lines out of Naples for several
hours.

Garbo got a friendly letter from Axel Munthe inviting her
to come to see him. She had liked his book and his letter
showed Munthe, who had been the benefactor of so many,
was then a man broken in health and totally blind. She waited
on the terrace and he was led up to her, leaning on a nurse's

arm. Garbo was deeply moved by the sight and her voice sounded strange as she greeted him. Munthe ran his fingers lightly across her face and, recognizing her, exclaimed, "How happy you've made me by coming."

Garbo couldn't speak because of her tears.

Some weeks later, she and Stokowski drove by car from Ravello to Sweden, where all went well as long as they stayed at Garbo's country place near Gnesta. It was midsummer, they lived outdoors and walked to the market in Gnesta for their fresh vegetables. As soon as they showed themselves in the capital, however, their peace was at an end. The reporters were not content to waylay them in hotel corridors and at shop counters, but made barricades of hay on the main road into the city to force them out of their car. But Stokowski refused to be stopped; he drove the car right off the road and into a field, where it turned over without injury to either of them. The poor desperate man ran his hands through his white mane, stamped his feet and gesticulated. Hadn't he been decent enough to give the press a long interview only a week before? Yes indeed, but he had talked about everything except Garbo and—well, "You see, Mr. Stokowski!" Mr. Stokowski didn't see and refused to accept their argument. As a result he got a bad write-up.

Stokowski could not stay away as long as Garbo, and he returned to the United States alone. A short time later, he announced his forthcoming marriage to Gloria Vanderbilt, and the disappointed press came to the conclusion that Garbo, who had been besieged with offers of marriage throughout her career, was unlucky in love. What an anticlimax to such a long honeymoon!

Chapter 19

TRAGEDIENNE—COMEDIENNE—
CRAZY ARTISTE

THE only person to take it calmly was Garbo herself, and her Swedish friends insist that it never was her intention to marry Stokowski. Certainly she had seldom been so gay as in those days when she lived for a time in the city itself.

Her address she kept to herself. One night, after a dinner Mimi Pollack gave for her and other former students at the Royal Dramatic, the men insisted on seeing her home. Garbo told them she was staying at Grand Hotel. They dropped her there. Garbo went in through one door and out another and took a taxi back to her one-room flat in Östermalm, where no one had the faintest idea who the new tenant was.

It was at this dinner that someone remembered Fingal and Agaton, two imaginary rabbits with whose adventures Garbo used to regale her fellow students. Agaton was pure white and big and silly; Fingal brown, small and clever. Now, after all these years, they wanted to know what had befallen them.

"Agaton is no more," Garbo said darkly. "He strayed into

a neighbor's garden, where they mistook him for a wild rabbit and shot him—which was queer, as he didn't look in the least wild."

"No, he was pretty easygoing, wasn't he?"

"Well, he was getting on and beginning to get a bit corpulent."

"And Fingal?"

"Oh, he's married and has grown-up children."

Metro had now persuaded Garbo to make one more film. She had agreed to this on condition that it was a pure comedy part. In Hollywood they smiled at Metro's indulgence—it was like letting a Wagnerian singer do popular hits. But those who were not aware that Garbo possessed a sense of humor most certainly didn't know her.

Ernst Lubitsch did, and he and Garbo had often talked of doing something together. Garbo admired Lubitsch. When she saw his *Love Parade* with Maurice Chevalier and Jeanette MacDonald she had clapped her hands delightedly, then driven to his house with an armful of roses and thrust them at him, exclaiming: *"Oh, Ernst, was für ein Film—ich gratuliere!"* Lubitsch, who had a houseful of guests, was delighted and asked her in, but she would not enter. They must have a talk some day, she said.

Garbo would have liked to make a film of the play *Tovarishch* which she had seen in Stockholm, but Warner Brothers had bought the rights for Claudette Colbert. This, however, gave Lubitsch an idea, and he and Walter Reich worked out a comedy based on a story by Melchior Lengyel, which they called *Ninotchka*. It was an unusually witty story— even for Lubitsch.

Ninotchka comes to Paris, a fanatical agent sent to reprimand three Communist officials for their slackness and remind them of their duties. "Love is a romantic explanation of a chemical process," she gravely tells the crestfallen trio. But she soon discovers for herself that Paris is a dangerous city, especially when represented by a young French count in the person of Melvyn Douglas. He manages to get her to a *chambre séparée*, where she gradually melts. There is one enchanting line when she is beginning to give way; she says slowly nodding her head, "Chemically we are agreed."

Garbo's acting made Lubitsch beam with delight.

Garbo's other partner was Ina Claire—now Gilbert's widow—and people had anticipated a certain tension in the meeting between the two. If any rivalry remained, it was thought it could only benefit the film in which they fight each other for Melvyn Douglas. But Ina Claire also had a sense of humor. The two became great friends from the start. Ina had been in variety and used to amuse Garbo in the intervals by tap-dancing. Garbo became intrigued, watched attentively, and one morning her dresser, Hazel, found her in front of the long mirror in her dressing room doing peculiar things with her feet.

Acting in a comedy seemed to lighten the burden of working and to make Garbo more relaxed. Lubitsch's wife and daughter were to fly to Europe for a holiday and one morning Lubitsch complained that he was not going to be able to see them off, as the plane left in the afternoon. Hearing this, Garbo said, "But of course you can! We'll work in the evening instead."

"Will you really do that?"

"Naturally."

And so they did. It was not difficult for Garbo to get the technicians to agree; at the end of every film she used to make them presents of whisky, cigarettes and chocolate and they loved her.

Heyman, the man who wrote the music for *Ninotchka*, was present while the film was made, but having been told how Garbo reacted to strangers in the studio, he fled whenever he saw her. One day Garbo said, "Who's that man who runs and hides whenever I look at him? Tell him to come and introduce himself."

Many people think that easy laughter came into Garbo's life with Gayelord Hauser.

Hauser's first approach was a fiasco. Garbo was reserved and unapproachable. But Hauser persisted in seeking her out and talking about himself and his system—incidentally he was an excellent advertisement for it. As a boy Hauser had been a wretched specimen. Tubercular and given up by his doctors, he had not only cured himself but developed a magnificent physique with broad shoulders and the agility of an expert gymnast. Garbo became more and more intrigued by this cocky youth of fifty who glowed with vitality and self-confidence. He had already performed miracles with some film big shots. Stars with fading sex appeal and dwindling fan mail had acquired a fresh radiance, through him. Famous names with diminished reputations and self-confidence had been cured by his yoghurt and spinach. He had brought happiness to the millionaires of Florida and had acquired a considerable fortune and an international reputation.

He intensified his attacks on Garbo. He succeeded in gaining her attention by doing the opposite of what everyone else did by going against her on essential points. If she wanted to be alone, he saw to it that she was plunged into a big party; a headache, he said, vanished if one drank a cocktail of grapefruit, honey and wheat germ. His cure for fatigue was a walk instead of going to bed. One ought to be healthy and sociable; that was the only way one could get anything out of life.

He and she used to lie and sun-bathe on the beach. In order to smooth out the wrinkles on one's face and neck, a person's feet must be twelve inches higher than his head. "Relax," Hauser told her. "Remember that relaxation is youth; one must learn to accept one's youth, which is one's true self."

On one occasion they were joined by an elderly man, a friend of Hauser who, strangely enough, did not know Garbo. They bathed and afterward Hauser asked the man what he thought of his friend. "Very nice, but to be frank I should have thought you could have got yourself something a bit better." When Hauser told this to Garbo, she laughed. "There you are," she said, "it's no use your stuffing me with calf's liver and sun cocktails; it doesn't make me any better-looking."

After her friendship with Stokowski, who was a rabid vegetarian, Garbo had as good as forsworn meat. Hauser put an end to that; a little meat was good, provided it was accompanied by green vegetables, yoghurt and brewer's yeast. Such a diet made one feel good and gay. If you wanted to be even gayer, you could drink a glass of champagne. If you wanted to live to a hundred, that was all right too; you only had to accept his gospel and preferably its apostle as well. One of his girl friends was seventy and still startlingly youthful.

There was a report in the press that he and Garbo were engaged and the wedding bells might start ringing at any moment. But not a chime was heard. Garbo had wearied again.

Ninotchka was a great success, greater than either *Camille* or *Conquest*, which were considered too serious, so Metro commissioned the playwright S. N. Behrman to adapt a comedy of Ludwig Fulda's into a crazy story for Garbo. *Two-*

faced Woman was an unfortunate speculation and an absolute failure. Lubitsch had been clever enough to let Garbo
be what came natural to her, an unpolished girl, blunt and
with a warm heart, and her own heaviness fitted in with the
Russian melancholy. In *Two-faced* Woman, however, she
was an empty doll who mechanically moved in a script that
called for a farce technique Garbo did not possess. She could
not identify herself with the part and whatever George Cukor
did, he could not induce the right mood in her. The longer
they filmed, the more people wondered how M-G-M could
have wanted to make her a Rosalind Russell or Katharine
Hepburn. Garbo has a sense of humor, but not a sense of
the ridiculous.

All *Two-faced* Woman achieved was to shock Garbo's public by showing her in a diaphanous nightie and a bathing suit,
the latter a garment she had not worn since playing a bathing
beauty in her first Swedish film.

Chapter 20

RESTLESS

WHY, one wonders, was *Two-faced Woman* in 1941 her last film? It wasn't a good film and she must certainly have regretted making it, but M-G-M denied that it was a financial failure. As with all Garbo films, the box-office returns were good, especially in Europe, which had always been Garbo's best market, so it wasn't that. The probable reason is that when World War II broke out it was no longer possible to export films and Garbo's market was gone. At the end of the war Garbo considered herself too old.

Yet letters still come to the M-G-M offices from admirers all over the world begging for new Garbo films, and in the film museum in New York she is the star most asked about. She herself seems to doubt the public interest in her. When Hedda Hopper, who played Garbo's sister in *As you Desire Me*, met her recently and asked why she did not make any more films, Garbo said, "Do you think people would still want to see me?"

Louis B. Mayer tried to tempt her into making a comeback by offering her $250,000 for one film, leaving the choice entirely up to her. Even if she didn't like any of the scripts, the money was to be hers.

They had been thinking of redoing *Flesh and the Devil*. But no, Garbo wasn't interested, nor were any other of their suggestions more favorably received. Her refusal of a quarter of a million dollars made a great impression on Mayer.

Some weeks after this incident Garbo went to see her friend Cecil Beaton, who had photographed all the Hollywood stars except her. Beaton naturally thought that she had just come to take him off to lunch somewhere and was quite surprised when she said, "It's a pity you're such a famous photographer; I'm thinking of going abroad and . . ."

Beaton guessed her dilemma. "I see, and you need a passport photo."

She did not want to go to an ordinary photographer, who undoubtedly would have exploited her name; and that is how Beaton's famous Garbo picture came about.

She was accompanied on the voyage by George Schlee, a middle-aged businessman of Russian origin. At the inevitable interview, Schlee denied that he was Garbo's "boy friend." He was happily married to Valentine, the New York fashion designer, and he didn't want any fuss. "Why was he escorting Miss Garbo?" As far as he was concerned, he said, he was going on a business trip. Garbo and he were good friends and as they chanced to be traveling in the same ship it was natural that they should see something of each other. But the reporters thought that he protested too much and their cameras clicked eagerly.

"Gentlemen," said Mr. Schlee, "if you intend to publish

those pictures, you must promise to mention me as Mrs. Valentine's husband."

At Stockholm, Garbo was met by her old friend Max Gumpel, who drove her straight out to his country place, where his daughter acted as hostess. Garbo was seen quite a good deal in restaurants, sometimes with both Gumpel and Schlee, whose business trip to Paris had apparently been postponed. Gumpel was indeed one of her oldest friends. This is his own account of how they met:

> In the infancy of films PUB must have been the first Swedish concern to use a film for advertising. The idea in those days was just to show mother, father and children going shopping, in this case in the various departments of PUB. The little boy in this film happened to be my sister's child, and, of course, I went to PUB to see the film being made. I may be forgiven for having paid more attention to a beautiful girl who was one of the staff taking part in the film. She was lovely. I invited her home to dinner. She came and I remember that we had crown artichokes, which were new to her.
>
> After that we met quite often, and I willingly admit that I was very keen on her, so much indeed that I gave her a tiny gold ring with a tiny diamond in it. There was no mistaking the genuineness of her delight at it, and she flattered me by thinking that it gleamed like one of the British crown jewels.
>
> A few years passed and we parted, good friends as we had always been. I went one way and married another girl, and she went to the theatrical school and then out into the world and became the big star she was intended to be.
>
> Ten years passed; I was divorced. The star came to Sweden. One day I received a phone call at the office. A woman's voice asked if I would dine with an old friend. She was mystifying, but eventually told me who she was. At that I became very cautious, for it could easily have been someone trying to make a fool of me. Anyway, I asked the voice to put on an evening

frock and come and dine in my home. When she said that she did not possess such a thing, I told her just to make herself as beautiful as she could. She came—and it was she. The only jewelry she had on was my little diamond ring. Then I did think that the diamond shone like those in the British crown; but she lent it that brilliance.

The film companies continued to tempt her, but Garbo preferred to go to London, where Cecil Beaton acted as her escort. There too she made the acquaintance of Princess Margaret at a party at the Duchess of Devonshire's. She was presented to her by Cecil Beaton.

Beaton did his best to make her visit to London pleasant, but apparently it was not easy. "She isn't interested in anything," he said with a sigh to some reporters; "as difficult to adapt herself as an invalid." But he also spoke of her "great fund of emotional resources."

Back in Stockholm, she was with some friends when someone mentioned the film offers she had been getting. She said, "Well, I think Stockholm is nicer than Hollywood."

"So you'll stay at home now?"

"I don't know where my home is."

She had never been to the north of Sweden and wanted to go there on a motor trip. "I want to go right up to the midnight sun."

"It's a long way."

"I've the time now."

But she didn't take it. After visiting the Riviera, she joined up with Baron Erich Rothschild and went touring with him in Austria. Rothschild was then over sixty, an authority on art, and usually took Garbo to the exhibitions in New York, where she returned late that fall. The assembled reporters wished her welcome; she was now an American citizen.

"Are you happy to be back in the U.S.A.?"

"When one has been so long in a country one grows to like it."

"As a matter of fact, Miss Garbo, has any romance come into your life while abroad?"

She laughed. "Isn't life always full of romance?"

Then of course the rumors started about films she was to make, companies she was going to start.

Then came her inheritance, through the death of an old invalid who had lived in a ramshackle cottage in Michigan. To everyone's surprise he left a will, sealed and formal, to the effect that "I, Edgard H. Donne, bequeath my entire fortune of $75,000, inclusive of securities and jewelry, to Greta Lovisa Gustafsson, by profession film star and known under the name of Garbo. Should she agree to become my wife, my house and land similarly go to Greta Lovisa Donne."

Garbo has now sold her own house in California and her country place in Frutuna with all its contents. Her belongings were auctioned; the phonograph went for ten shillings and a big grandfather clock for next to nothing. Now she lives in a hotel in New York, when she isn't traveling about the world. Presumably she considers this way of life best suited to her restlessness, which seems to have increased since she stopped making pictures.

What is the cause?

There is one part that she has never been able to master and which she is now forced to play every day, that of Greta Garbo. She speaks several languages, can talk about books and art, and is undoubtedly aware that kings and commoners are alike before the Lord. Yet when Garbo makes an entrance, Greta Gustafsson still shrinks and wants to hold back. The thing that saves her from serious consequences because of this dual personality is that Greta Gustafsson isn't merely shy, but also has a robust sense of humor inherited from her farmer ancestors. She can laugh at the myth of the prima donna weary of fame, trailing from continent to continent. The mysterious Garbo exists only in the public imagination.

Chapter 21

THE CONCEPT "GARBO"

GARBO appeared on the scene at the right psychological moment and filled this new need. Men said, "She is just what we yearn for, not too feminine, but more like ourselves"; while women, who had entered the labor market, had begun to feel uncomfortable wearing long hair and long skirts. They said, "She is our ideal, that's how we want to look and be." They were attracted by her masculinity; men by her sensualism. She walked like a man, swinging her shoulders, was big-boned and flat-chested; her all but nonexistent curves corresponded to no measurements of any classic Venus. She was not graceful, yet she had the strength and agility of an animal.

Was she beautiful?

Scarcely, in the accepted meaning of the word. There are plenty of mannequins, chorus girls and actresses with more beautiful features and limbs, but they do not entrance us the same way as did Garbo, whose beauty is more a matter of experience than perception.

Similarly, it is more her personality that grips us than her art. She is a face, never a mask; therein lie both her strength and her weakness. She had to be allowed to subjectivize her parts. Whenever she has had to be a type, she has failed; you could see that she was blindly following her director's instructions and the camera ruthlessly revealed all the falsity of the part.

The secret of her acting is that she has been able to be herself. She has been able to portray a part of life in such a way that it retains its original liberating force. A great actress does not act, she reveals herself. Her nature is so rich that she is universal.

The expression she achieves is not conscious, but a fortunate harmony of mind, heart and nerves. The dark and unspoken with its rich possibilities appeals to something within her and sets her ethereal genius vibrating. She is neither ingenue nor vamp, flapper nor grande dame, but all women in one—wrapped in the mystery of the eternal Eve. She is the nymph who entices but will not let herself be caught; her victims glimpse her beneath a street lamp in the mist, while riding on the steppe in the twilight, through the swirling smoke on a railway platform just as the train is moving off.

Her face is pure but experienced, and what she experiences is harmonious with her nature, as inevitable as rain or a natural catastrophe. When the storm has passed, her being is like a meadow after rain, like the sea after a night of storm—refreshed and reborn, quiet and tested, but with its depths untouched. Her eroticism is extreme and satisfies both the connoisseur and the Philistine's need of the unusual which is denied him in his banal marriage. The ordinary husband imagines himself with Garbo and thinks, "With some other wife, what sensational things wouldn't I have accomplished!"

She maintains a natural balance even in the scenes of greatest passion and never becomes hysterical. Nor is she coquettish in the ordinary sense; there is a masculine element in her manner. She attracts as much with her personality, as with her sex appeal.

Can one imagine a person less ordinary than Garbo, whose desires, even when young, were never the usual ones: a home with husband and children, a country cottage, a car of recent model? Her objectives have always been unconventional. She is a living protest against bourgeois materialism, against the hustle and bustle of the age, against the collectivism that wants to wipe out all individuality. Do convention and custom exist to protect real cultural values? As often as not, they only serve to hide what is warped and defective in our way of life. Garbo is a reply to cowardly humdrum routine and mediocrity. She has shown that she has the courage to live her own life.

But people have always found it difficult to stomach someone who is different, who has the courage not only to choose his or her company, but even to do without any. According to the average person, there must be something wrong with someone who does that. Either he or she is afraid to meet others for fear of revealing some mental or physical defect, or else he is conceited, and the only reason for that is—here follows an eloquent gesture toward the speaker's brow. When the person concerned is a woman, and, despite her conceit or defect, passes from glory to glory, it makes people angry and they begin to throw smoke bombs to drive her out of her isolation.

Garbo has had to endure the treatment normally meted

out to those who are unusual. People will without protest respect the wishes of the writer, composer, painter who isolates himself and whose work makes him inaccessible, yet they take it as a matter of course that the actor or actress, rehearsals or performance over, will continue to display his or her prowess in the circle of his friends and acquaintances. Why doesn't one ask the artist to do a little sketch when he's under one's roof, the writer to write a short story in which all one's guests will figure, or the composer to write a tune that one and one's guests can all dance to? The art of the actor is a matter of subtle adaptation to partner, director, and the public. He, or she, is compelled to strain nerves to the breaking point; and when the long working day is over seek rest from declaiming and aping.

Garbo achieved her tremendous reputation without ever making herself common. Many people have taken her refusals to let herself be photographed or to sell kisses at charity bazaars as personal affronts. One is comfortably installed in front of the fire with wife and children and a safe income, everything nice and well ordered, yet she grudges one something to talk about! If she really has to be like that, then it's her duty to give her isolation an interesting atmosphere. Other stars, for example, have installed alarm systems costing thousands of dollars that go into action the moment anyone tries to approach; one bought a new watchdog for every film she made, naming the dog after the film. That was all right, because it gave the public something to talk about. Others will gladly tell you what brand of corset makes them look slimmest and what cigarette they smoke with their morning coffee. Why should Garbo keep everything to herself like that?

Everything points to Garbo's being born with a very

strong sensibility. She all too obviously doubts her own abil-
ities, an unusual attribute in actors, but not in other artists.
While in Hollywood she wrote to a friend in Stockholm,
"Sometimes I get an awful longing to be born all over again
so as to get away from this feeling of being nothing." She
easily became depressed and withdrew within herself. "My
best company I find in myself," she wrote when she was fourteen. Three years later, when she embarked on her acting career, she had felt inferior because of her insufficient schooling.
She said to her friend Eva, "The father of one of them
[the students] is a mayor, another's is a professor; they all know
languages and can play the piano. I don't know anything."
These feelings persisted even when she was a world-famous
star. "I can't go about and see people and I live like a nun."
Her isolation increased people's curiosity. "Now I've become
'mysterious' just because I won't go out and amuse myself. . . ."

The person has yet to be born whose nervous system
could remain unaffected by the impact of the brutal curiosity
of the whole world. Here one can speak of reciprocal effects.
The farther Garbo withdrew, the greater became the interest
in her, and when the legend around her began to assume really
gigantic proportions, she was forced to take desperate meas-
ures to defend her seclusion.

Old acquaintances have complained of how reserved she
grew after she became famous. It is common knowledge that
people try to exploit those to whom fame and riches come.
While she was a star Garbo received thousands of letters asking for financial help—and not always asking; sometimes
threatening. On occasion the approach was even more direct.
The characters in one of her early films included two street-
walkers; the director had engaged two professional call girls

to play the parts. In an unguarded moment during production, they came up to Garbo and said in low but emphatic tones, "Miss Garbo, if you don't pay so-and-so much, things will happen to you that you won't find very pleasant."

Could one really expect Garbo to open her arms to all who approached her? If she had, she would have long since been trampled and suffocated by her fame.

Stars of considerably less luster than Garbo who were sent out on publicity tours have been so exhausted by all the commotion that they have been unable to give intelligent answers to all the questions asked. One male star, a man with a strong physique, announced at the end of such a tour that he would rather make four films one after the other than do such a thing again. And is it not often so, that the greater the talent, the more sensitive the person concerned, the more inclined to shrink from having anything to do with the impertinent and pushing?

Garbo asked for neither appreciation nor admiration, merely the same consideration she showed to others. Being absolutely unaffected herself, she could only stand people who were themselves without conceit, and when she suspected people of having preconceived ideas about herself, she felt uncomfortable and disappeared. She could not afford to lose any of the dear-bought solitude and composure that she needed so badly for her next part. Hers was the artistic nature's jealousy of real life.

She has said that she felt unable as a private person to live up to the public's expectations of her. One evening she and a friend went to a restaurant for supper, but they had to leave before they had time even to give their order, because people kept coming up to touch her. All over the world, when she appeared on the screen, she set up a wave of sensuality. Men and women worshiped her image, and each one filled in the detail as far as their imaginations allowed. Thus, whenever she appeared among them, people lost their heads and came rushing up to verify that she had substance, was of flesh and blood. And because this was so, she fled in order that millions should not feel themselves duped and in their disappointment tear her to pieces. But people weren't able to understand her motives and so flung stones at the fleeing figure: haughty, materialistic, acquisitive, mean!

She has summed up all her film work as having "acted in a couple of good pictures." Not all film stars are equally unassuming. Louis B. Mayer looked greatly surprised when she refused to accept a quarter of a million dollars. That same sum has been offered her to appear on television and she has refused it. In 1932 the Beverly Hills Bank failed. She had money in it, but took the loss philosophically. She has no interest in clothes and wears no jewelry. Is she a materialist without interests? Stokowski is not the only one to bear witness to her love of music. Françoise Rosay has told how Garbo always tried to get her to play Debussy and Fauré. She reads good books and is sufficiently interested in painting to have acquired several works of the French Impressionists. She is quite indifferent to honors and distinctions. When the King of Sweden awarded her his country's highest distinction, *Litteris et Artibus,* the Swedish ambassador to the United States had a very difficult job reaching her. Is she even ambitious? Scarcely. She doesn't know what jealousy is and never listens to gossip.

Is she stupid? Could a stupid person behave as she has? François Mauriac, Louis Bromfield, Walter Hasenclever, have considered her intelligent. And emotionally? Do we need more evidence than her twenty-seven films that she is superbly equipped emotionally?

And what of her relations to her fellow beings? She feels compassion, but not sympathy in the sentimental sense of the word. She has always taken care of her family and she gave Finland a large sum of money during the Winter War. As a child she knew what real poverty was and the fact of having to work hard for a living impressed on her the value of money. On one of her visits to Sweden she was invited to attend a charity performance to help indigent actors. She telegraphed in reply, "The cause does not interest me." When a rather feminine actor whom she knew once asked her help in getting him into a film she said, "Do you mean that I should be your pimp?"

Her detractors call her dull as granite and cold as an icicle. She is typically Swedish: tall as a pine, melancholy as winter twilight. Such blood does not flow freely and that is reflected in her features; but when they are lighted up by a smile, they remind one of a snow-capped mountain glistening in the sun.

A number of her Hollywood acquaintances have called her egocentric. She could come barging in on them at the most unexpected hours, yet she herself always refused to receive visitors who came without warning or prior arrangement. Often she would send a message that she was not at home, merely because she was interested in the book she was reading or was busy preparing the next day's scenes. That is selfish, seen from the bourgeois point of view; but aren't all artists egoistic, don't they have to be in order to create? Garbo is not an author, yet her attitude is quite similar to that of many great writers. A world-famous author once invited some fifty guests to dinner. They came and waited and waited for their host. Finally the great writer's servant ventured to knock on his door to say, "The guests are waiting!" "Let them wait," said the great man, "I'm working."

Garbo's flight from the public has been called a smart publicity stunt, yet if you consider her conduct, you will see that she has accepted what Goethe has written about the difficulties of being famous: *Ruhm—nur mit Handschuhn fass ich dich an!* (Fame—only with gloves can I hold you.) The artist needs a certain distance and detachment not only from fame, but also from life. Life is rather like a flower; its scent can become coarse and vulgar, if you hold it too close to your nose. The artist flees from life in order to win it. He knows how to hunger, knows that he must never eat his fill—and out of that hunger for life he creates life.

In his famous essay on "Social Life and Solitude," Emerson points out that if there is something valuable about a person, Nature will usually protect it by making him impossible for social life. The masses are the *vulgus* which the artistic person must keep at a distance in order to be able to hear the music within himself. As long as he can keep the tone of this music pure and clear, he is never utterly alone.

Garbo's life has been full of the things that other women spend their lives dreaming about: beauty, success, wealth, and fame. Still she does not seem satisfied. Perhaps because "living" does not mean the same to her as it does to others. She has the artist's eternal longing for what she cannot achieve, cannot perform.

But one thing is certain. Whenever the history of the cinema is written, one name always shines more brilliantly than any other: Greta Garbo.

Appendix

Garbo's Films in Europe

1. Among the extras in John Brunius' *En Lyckoriddare* were Greta and Alva Gustafsson.

2. PUB'S advertising film, 1921. Producer: Hasse W. Tullberg. Director: Captain Lars Ring.

3. Advertising film for Co-operative Society of Stockholm. Producer: Fribergs filmbyra. Director: Captain Lars Ring.

4. *Luffar-Petter*
   Author, director and producer: Erik A. Petschler. Première: December 26, 1922.

Brandlöjtnant Erik Silverjälm } Erik A. Petschler	
Max August Pettersson }	
(Luffar-Petter)	
Greta Nordberg	Greta Gustafsson
Kaptenen	Helmer Larsson
Police Commissioner	Fredrik Olsson

5. *Gösta Berling's Saga*
   Script: Mauritz Stiller and Ragnar Hyltén-Cavallius after Selma Lagerlöf's novel. Cameraman: Julius Jaenzon. Pro-

ducer: Svensk Filmindustri. Director: Mauritz Stiller. Première: Part I, March 10, 1924, Part II, March 17, 1924.

Gösta Berling	Lars Hanson
Mrs. Samzelius	Gerda Lundequist
Major Samzelius	Otto Elg-Lundberg
Melchior Sinclair	Sixten Malmerfeldt
Gustafva Sinclair	Karin Swanström
Countess Elisabeth Dohna	Greta Garbo

6. *Die Freudlose Gasse*
Script: Willy Haas after Hugo Bettauer's novel. Cameraman: Guido Seeber. Producer: Sofar Film. Director: G. W. Pabst. Première in Berlin, May 18, 1925, in Stockholm, September 28, 1925.

Franz Rumfort	Jaro Furth
Butcher	Werner Krauss
Maria Lechner	Asta Nielsen
Greta Rumfort	Greta Garbo
Mrs. Griefer	Valeska Gert
Lieutenant Davy	Einar Hanson

Garbo's Films in U.S.A.
All produced by M-G-M

1. *The Torrent*
Script: Dorothy Farnum, after a novel by Blasco-Ibañez. Cameraman: William Daniels. Director: Monta Bell. Première in U.S.A., February 21, 1926.

Leonora	Greta Garbo
Don Rafel Brull	Ricardo Cortez
Remedios	Gertrude Olmstead
Pedro Moreno	Edward Connelly
Cupido	Lucien Littlefield

2. *The Temptress*
Script: Dorothy Farnum, after a novel by Blasco-Ibañez.

Cameraman: Tony Gaudio. Director: Mauritz Stiller and Fred Niblo. Première, U.S.A., October 10, 1926.

Elena	Greta Garbo
Robledo	Antonio Moreno
Manos Duros	Roy d'Arcy
Fontenoy	Marc McDermott
Canterac	Lionel Barrymore

3. *The Flesh and the Devil*
Script: Benjamin Glazer, after Hermann Sudermann's novel, *Es War*. Cameraman: William Daniels. Director: Clarence Brown. Première in U.S.A., January 9, 1927.

Felicitas von Kletzingk	Greta Garbo
Leo von Sellinthin	John Gilbert
Ulrich von Kletzingk	Lars Hanson
Hertha Prochwitz	Barbara Kent
Kutowski	William Orlamond

4. *Love*
Script: Frances Marion, after Leo Tolstoi's novel *Anna Karenina*. Cameraman: William Daniels. Director: Edmund Goulding. Première in U.S.A., November 29, 1927.

Anna Karenina	Greta Garbo
Vronsky	John Gilbert
Grand Duke	George Fawcett
Grand Duchess	Emily Fitzroy
Karenin	Brandon Hurst

5. *The Divine Woman*
Script: Dorothy Farnum, after Gladys Unger's play *Starlight*. Cameraman: Oliver Marsh. Director: Victor Sjöström. Première in U.S.A., January 14, 1928.

Marianne	Greta Garbo
Lucien	Lars Hanson
M. Legrande	Lowell Sherman
Mme. Pigonier	Polly Moran
Mme. Zizi Rouck	Dorothy Cumming

6. *The Mysterious Lady*
Script: Bess Meredyth, after Ludwig Wolff's novel, *War in the Dark*. Cameraman: William Daniels. Director: Fred Niblo. Première in U.S.A., August 4, 1928.

Tania	Greta Garbo
Karl	Conrad Nagel
General Alexandroff	Gustav von Seyffertitz
Colonel von Raden	Edward Connelly
Max	Albert Pollet

7. *A Woman of Affairs*
Script: Bess Meredyth, after Michael Arlen's novel *The Green Hat*. Cameraman: William Daniels. Director: Clarence Brown. Première, in U.S.A., January 19, 1929.

Diana	Greta Garbo
Neville	John Gilbert
Hugh	Lewis Stone
David	John Mack Brown
Geoffrey	Douglas Fairbanks, Jr.

8. *Wild Orchids*
Script: Hans Kräly, Richard Schayer and Willis Goldbeck, after a suggestion by John Colton. Cameraman: William Daniels. Director: Sidney Franklin. Première in U.S.A., March 30, 1929.

Lillie Sterling	Greta Garbo
John Sterling	Lewis Stone
Prince De Grace	Nils Asther

9. *The Single Standard*
Script: Josephine Lovett, after a novel by Adela Rogers St. Johns. Cameraman: Oliver Marsh. Director: John S. Robertson. Première in U.S.A., July 27, 1929.

Arden Stuart	Greta Garbo
Packy Cannon	Nils Asther
Tommy Hewlett	John Mack Brown
Mercedes	Dorothy Sebastian
Ding Stuart	Lane Chandler

10. *The Kiss*
Script: Hans Kräly, after an idea of George M. Saville.
Cameraman: William Daniels. Director: Jacques Feyder.
Première in U.S.A., November 15, 1929.

Mme. Irène Guarry	Greta Garbo
André	Conrad Nagel
M. Guarry	Anders Randolf
Lassalle	Holmes Herbert
Pierre	Lew Ayres

11. *Anna Christie*
Script: Frances Marion, after Eugene O'Neill's play. Cameraman: William Daniels. Director: Clarence Brown. Première
in U.S.A., March 14, 1930.

Anna	Greta Garbo
Matt Burke	Charles Bickford
Marthy	Marie Dressler
Chris	George F. Marion
Johnny the Priest	James T. Mack

12. *Romance*
Script: Bess Meredyth and Edwin Justus Mayer, after Edward
Sheldon's play. Cameraman: William Daniels. Director: Clar-
ence Brown. Première in U.S.A., August 22, 1930.

Rita Cavallini	Greta Garbo
Cornelius Van Tuyl	Lewis Stone
Tom Armstrong	Gavin Gordon
Harry	Elliott Nugent
Susan Van Tuyl	Florence Lake

13. *Inspiration*
Script: Gene Markey. Cameraman: William Daniels. Director:
Clarence Brown, Première in U.S.A., February 6, 1931.

Yvonne	Greta Garbo
André	Robert Montgomery
Delval	Lewis Stone
Lulu	Marjorie Rambeau
Odette	Judith Vosselli

14. *Susan Lenox: Her Fall and Rise.* Script: Wanda Tuchock, after David Graham Phillip's novel. Cameraman: William Daniels. Director: Robert Z. Leonard. Première in U.S.A., October 16, 1931.

Susan Lenox	Greta Garbo
Rodney	Clark Gable
Ohlin	Jean Hersholt
Burlingham	John Miljan
Mondstrum	Alan Hale

15. *Mata Hari*
Script: Benjamin Glazer and Leo Birinski. Cameraman: William Daniels. Director: George Fitzmaurice. Première in U.S.A., December 31, 1931.

Mata Hari	Greta Garbo
Lt. Alexis Rosanoff	Ramon Novarro
General Shubin	Lionel Barrymore
Adriani	Lewis Stone
Dubois	C. Henry Gordon

16. *Grand Hotel*
Script: William A. Drake, after Vicki Baum's novel. Cameraman: William Daniels. Director: Edmund Goulding. Première in U.S.A., April 12, 1932.

Grusinskaya	Greta Garbo
Baron von Gaigern	John Barrymore
Flaemmchen	Joan Crawford
Preysing	Wallace Beery
Otto Kringelein	Lionel Barrymore

17. *As You Desire Me*
Script: Gene Markey, after Luigi Pirandello's play. Cameraman: William Daniels. Director: George Fitzmaurice. Première in U.S.A., June 2, 1932.

Maria (Zara)	Greta Garbo
Count Bruno Varelli	Melvyn Douglas
Carl Salter	Erich von Stroheim
Tony Boffie	Owen Moore
Mme. Mantari	Hedda Hopper

18. *Queen Christina*
Script: Salka Viertel and H. M. Harwood, after an idea of
Salka Viertel and Margaret F. Levine. Cameraman: William
Daniels. Director: Rouben Mamoulian. Première in U.S.A.,
December 26, 1933.

Queen Christina	Greta Garbo
Don Antonio de la Prada	John Gilbert
Magnus	Ian Keith
Axel Oxenstierna	Lewis Stone
Ebba Sparre	Elizabeth Young

19. *The Painted Veil*
Script: John Meehan, Salka Viertel and Edith Fitzgerald, after
Somerset Maugham's novel. Cameraman: William Daniels.
Director: Richard Boleslawsky. Première in U.S.A., Decem-
ber 7, 1934.

Katrin	Greta Garbo
Walter Fane	Herbert Marshall
Jack Townsend	George Brent
General Yu	Warner Oland
Herr Koerber	Jean Hersholt

20. *Anna Karenina*
Script: Clemence Dane, Salka Viertel and S. N. Behrman,
after Leo Tolstoi's novel. Cameraman: William Daniels.
Director: Clarence Brown. Première in U.S.A., August 30,
1935.

Anna Karenina	Greta Garbo
Vronsky	Frederic March
Sergei	Freddie Bartholomew
Kitty	Maureen O'Sullivan
Countess Vronsky	May Robson

21. *Camille*
Script: Zoë Akins, Frances Marion and James Hilton, after
Alexander Dumas' novel and play *La Dame aux Camélias*.
Cameraman: William Daniels. Director: George Cukor.
Première in U.S.A., January 22, 1937.

Marguerite	Greta Garbo
Armand	Robert Taylor
Monsieur Duval	Lionel Barrymore
Nichette	Elizabeth Allan
Nanine	Jessie Ralph

22. *Conquest*
Script: Samuel Hoffenstein, Salka Viertel and S. N. Behrman,
after the novel *Pani Walewska* by Waclaw Gasiorowski and a
dramatized version by Helen Jerome. Cameraman: Karl
Freund. Director: Clarence Brown. Première in U.S.A., November 4, 1937.

Marie Walewska	Greta Garbo
Napoleon	Charles Boyer
Talleyrand	Reginald Owen
Captain d'Ornano	Alan Marshal
Greve Walewska	Henry Stephenson

23. *Ninotchka*
Script: Charles Brackett, Billy Wilder and Walter Reisch,
after a story by Melchior Lengyel. Cameraman: William
Daniels. Director: Ernst Lubitsch. Première in U.S.A., November 9, 1939.

Ninotchka	Greta Garbo
Count Leon d'Algout	Melvyn Douglas
Duchess Swana	Ina Claire
Iranoff	Sig Rumann
Buljanoff	Felix Bressart
Kopalski	Alexander Granach

24. *Two-Faced Woman*
Script: S. N. Behrman, Salka Viertel and George Oppen-
heimer, after a play by Ludwig Fulda. Cameraman: Joseph

Ruttenberg. Director: George Cukor. Première in U.S.A., December 31, 1941.

Karin	Greta Garbo
Larry Blake	Melvyn Douglas
Griselda Vaughn	Constance Bennett
O. O. Miller	Roland Young
Dick Williams	Robert Sterling
Miss Ellis	Ruth Gordon
Miss Dunbar	Frances Carson
Dancer	Bob Alton

INDEX

251